Rec^d Sat 30/1/99 from RICHMANDS. — Surrey.

Rec^d Sat 30/1/99 from RICHMANDS. — Surrey.

FIVE STAR
FUTURES TRADES

FIVE STAR
FUTURES TRADES

The Premier System
for Trading the Biggest Market Moves

Colin Alexander

Windsor Books, Brightwaters, NY 11718

Published by Windsor Books
P.O. Box 280
Brightwaters, NY 11718

Manufactured in the United States of America

ISBN 0-930233-58-1

Acknowledgments

To my editor, Ruth Rodger, I owe an immense debt of gratitude. This book would not have appeared in its current form without her perceptive and constructive criticism, demanding standards and substantial assistance in writing.

A special thank you goes also to Julie Gray, who did much more than the basic mechanical job of setting the type and formatting. Her patience and good humor never flagged during the process.

I am also most appreciative of the support and encouragement of my publishers. They have a saying: Quality is more important than time! This maxim is applicable to all aspects of life but nowhere more so than to futures trading.

C.A.

Contents

Chapter 1

The Challenge of Finding
the Biggest Market Moves

In the oil industry the expression for a Prudhoe Bay-size oil discovery is an "elephant". The Five Star system searches for the futures market equivalent to elephants. It may find many trades that are no more than chipmunks and there will be the oil industry's equivalent of dry holes. But make no mistake about it! There are always elephants out there and it finds them! They are the trades that make futures trading truly worthwhile over time—and fun.

This book is for all futures traders seeking the most reliable way to make money consistently. It concentrates on how to look for the biggest market moves and how to trade them. Making money from big moves is infinitely more reliable than making money in small ones. Not only do you make more money on individual trades but the probabilities in favor of making big net profits over time are higher when trading the biggest market moves. The risk of loss is also generally lower.

Basic Requirements

You don't require a real-time quotation service to use this book but you do need a computer, a basic software program and access to end-of-day prices. With home computers now standard, supplementary costs for software and end-of-day prices should be insignificant when trading the Five Star system, even if you have only a small account. It is not necessary to watch markets during the day, although it is helpful to get market ranges shortly before the close for any market that you are in or which you are thinking of trading.

The Five Star system is straightforward to use, both for professionals and for traders new to the market. And even if you are new to the market, there is no point in aspiring to be anything but a professional—that is, a successful trader. There is no magic about professionalism. Some full-time traders who could be described as professionals don't make money and some part-time traders using a good system make money consistently.

Although the Five Star system is relatively simple to use, it is not simplistic. If you are starting with essentially no knowledge of futures trading, learning the system might be compared with learning to play bridge proficiently or learning to fly a small airplane.* You should be able to start making real-time trades on paper within a few days and real trades in the market within a couple of weeks or so, depending on how much time you can put into learning it.

Once you are familiar with the Five Star system, it should take only about five minutes to go through our daily market checklist to decide which markets may be worth looking at in more detail. Then the process of deciding on an entry, an exit or a hold, using the entry and exit checklists, should take about five minutes more for each market of interest. It is usually obvious from the daily market checklist and from the daily bar chart which markets, if any, require more detailed attention.

The Essence of the System

The Five Star system uses computer-based technical indicators that are familiar to most futures traders: MACD, stochastics and moving averages of several lengths. But it uses these indicators in some unfamiliar ways to find and follow trends, and to identify overbought and oversold conditions. The system also uses specific price patterns, sentiment indicators and other basic tools of technical analysis such as trend and channel lines.

"Five Star" connotes excellence. The Five Star system seeks to achieve excellent trades by:

1. identifying potential trades at an early stage of development through using specific computer-based indicators innovatively;

2. using an objective procedure to make decisions to enter and exit trades; and

3. requiring, in the decision-making procedure, that a net total of five indicators (confirming indicators minus negating indicators) qualify a market to trade, first on the weekly chart and then on the daily chart.

The Five Star system trades three kinds of market action:

1. *Established trends*: The system aims to buy low and sell high (or sell high and then buy low) within the existing boundaries of a bull or bear trend.

2. *Rapidly moving markets*—generally, the more rapidly moving, the better: The system trades on an initial strong move out of a trading range, as well as subsequently when price action suggests that the market is about to make another surge in the direction of the trend.

---

* This book does not discuss how futures trading is carried out by exchanges and brokers, what markets and contracts are traded, etc. Readers with no experience in futures trading may find it useful to consult a basic textbook on the futures industry, such as the Chicago Board of Trade's *Commodity Trading Manual* (Chicago: Board of Trade of the City of Chicago, frequently reprinted and updated.) This book is informative, readable and strongly recommended.

3.   *Major trend changes*: These trades involve use of many of the techniques for buying low and selling high within an established trend, plus certain further uses of the indicators. The system recognizes that there are important differences between market action at major lows and at major market tops. Bottoms usually require time to build a base, while tops usually occur more quickly.

The largest and fastest profits can be made when a bubble bursts at tops. The result of a bubble bursting is what we call a vacuum crash. While such moves are relatively rare—just a few each year—the results can be spectacular when our prime vacuum crash indicators come together to ride a wave down, like riding the crest of the big surf in Hawaii. As well, these indicators help to avoid getting caught in a long position on the wrong side of a market collapse.

An important benefit of the Five Star system is that it normally generates too many conflicts among the indicators to allow for entries into sideways markets that have limited potential for profit. It also contains a special class of entry and exit signals that we call stochastic/gap signals. Under certain conditions, they can signal an entry into a trade or an exit from a trade earlier than the regular Five Star signals.

Duration of Trades

Some Five Star trades may last for many weeks or months but involve several entries and exits. A vacuum crash trade may involve only one trade of perhaps a few days to two or three months. On the other hand, a trade may be liquidated or stopped out within a day or two of entry, or occasionally on the same day when circumstances change abruptly. The system is not specifically designed for position-trading, for staying in a market for weeks and months on end, although some of the best trades can last a very long time if they don't generate exit signals on the way.

The reality of futures markets is that even within strong trends there can be very great volatility. It is seldom reasonable to tolerate a retracement that amounts to several times one's margin money. We therefore liquidate when there are signals suggesting that a larger retracement could be starting. When the retracement shows through price action and the delivery of new entry signals that it has most likely ended, we normally reinstate the position. Usually it is possible to re-enter a position at a more favorable price than when it is liquidated, although not always.

These actions reflect one of the basic strategies on which the Five Star system is based: conserve profits, reduce risk and enter trades when the probabilities favor immediate continuation to a profit. Although the latter doesn't always happen, since a trade may still have to consolidate after an entry signal is given, many of the best trades go to an immediate profit.

Inevitably, the Five Star system does not catch every major move as it is starting. You don't have to catch markets at the beginning of a move, however, to make money. Almost all the biggest market moves, with the exception of some vacuum crash trades, provide new system entry signals later on, when it is possible to make an initial entry.

Why Seek the Biggest Trades?

Considerable discussion about trading in futures markets is concerned with the respective merits of trading futures with a longer-term or a shorter perspective. We find it more useful to focus on the potential value of trades rather than on time, which means seeking fewer but bigger trades. The argument, reduced to its simplest terms, is this. If you constantly risk a dollar to make fifty cents, you must be right an inordinate percentage of the time in order to make money after paying for commissions and slippage. If you risk a dollar with the prospect that sometimes you will make five or ten dollars, and succeed in doing so reasonably often, you are more likely to make profits, and possibly substantial profits, over time. The objective of the Five Star system and its trading strategies are to place traders in the latter position.

The challenge in accomplishing this objective is to try to distinguish between, say, a Corn trade having the potential to make five or ten cents and a Bond trade having the potential to make five full points. Generally, it is not any more difficult or time-consuming to identify a trade having major potential than it is to identify one having favorable characteristics for a quick flip. The only substantial difference required for finding big trades rather than small ones is that you must have the patience and discipline to stand aside from markets with small potential. Otherwise you can tie up capital, time, energy and psychological commitment so that you aren't able to take advantage of major opportunities when they occur.

The biggest futures market trade in recent memory was to be short the stock index futures during the 1987 crash. The Five Star system signaled the move, which took the Standard & Poor 500 Index down by almost $90,000 per contract from top to bottom in just a few weeks. About two-thirds of that move was reasonably available as profit.

Another huge trade signaled by the Five Star system was the crash of the British Pound in September 1992, when financier George Soros is said to have make a billion dollars in just a few weeks. Although he was undoubtedly trading a huge fund account, Chart 1.1 shows that this was nonetheless a very big trade.[*]

From September to December 1992, the Pound went from a high weekly close at 1.9600 to a low weekly close at 1.4100 or 55 full points (rounded), for a total value of $34,375 per contract. Assuming that only $25,000 of this amount was booked as profit (with no allowance for adding contracts on the way down, as Mr. Soros might well have done) and assuming equity of $6,000, or three times the exchange minimum margin, this trade produced, at a minimum, a return of more than 400 percent in less than three months.

In contrast, a computer trading system discussed in a special report on trading systems published by *Futures* Magazine in 1994 produced a hypothetical

---

[*] It has been said that this trade is not a good example of technical analysis because Mr. Soros's own trading helped to break the Pound and make the chart. Our view is that all charts are made by the actions of people and that this is no exception.

profit of 1,385 percent trading the British Pound. But to do this it required seven years and $16,025 in equity to trade one contract (dictated by seven consecutive losing trades and a maximum drawdown of $12,875).

Of course, it is guaranteed that there will be losses when trading futures and some of Mr. Soros's losses are known to have been large. However, a logical conclusion from Mr. Soros's experience with his Pound trade is clear: looking for bigger trades can produce much better results.

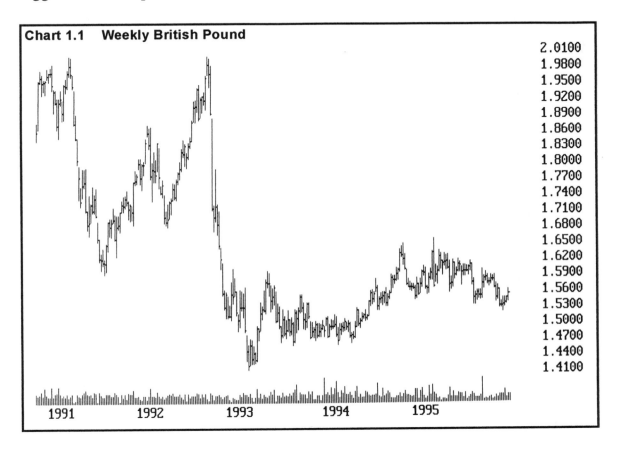

Chart 1.1 Weekly British Pound

Format

Each technical indicator that the Five Star System uses is described, and its action on weekly and daily charts is examined in brief, individual chapters. Inevitably, when a variety of technical indicators are discussed, the individual chapters may seem somewhat disjointed. The Five Star system comes together, though, in the checklists described in Chapters 17 to 19.

Discussing the technical indicators in individual chapters unavoidably makes it seem as if trading decisions are made on the basis of individual indicators. Not so. First, as mentioned, all of our indicators are brought together to be considered jointly in three checklists, which are used to monitor potential trades, and to enter and exit actual trades. Secondly, we believe that no single indicator can serve as a magic bullet in real-time trading. The complexities of futures trading plus the weaknesses inherent in all individual indicators make this impossible.

Even experienced traders familiar with the computer-based technical indicators that we use should look at the early chapters for the settings for these indicators and, equally important, for a discussion of the ways in which we use them, which vary markedly in some cases from common usage.

Readers less familiar with these indicators should find enough description for this book to stand alone as the source of information on their use. However, those interested in knowing more about the technical indicators we use can find further discussions on them in most of the more recent books on technical analysis. *Technical Traders Guide to Computer Analysis of the Futures Market* by Charles LeBeau and David W. Lucas contains particularly good discussions of these computer-based technical indicators plus the common mathematical formulas from which they are derived.[*]

In connection with the settings for the computer-based technical indicators, different software programs may produce somewhat different results from the same settings. These differences occur because the mathematical formulas used for technical studies are not standardised across the software industry. The Five Star system uses only two indicators that may produce somewhat different results in various software: moving average convergence/divergence (MACD) and stochastics. The system has enough cross references among indicators that small differences should not materially affect the delivery of signals.

We use the B.M.I. data feed and Ensign software with an I.B.M. compatible computer, and find this combination excellent. With services constantly changing and improving, the best guide to the availability of services and software are *Futures* magazine and *Stocks and Commodities*, which are available at major newsstands. As a general rule, the least elaborate and most economical services are best.

The subject matter of the chapters is grouped as follows:

Chapters 2 to 14 - Five Star computer-based technical indicators, price rule signals and other technical indicators for identifying trends, entries and exits.

Chapter 15 - Stops and capital management.

Chapter 16 - Summary of how to find the biggest and most reliable trades.

Chapters 17 to 19 - Daily market checklist, entry checklist and exit checklist.

Chapters 20 to 23 - Case studies of trades in each of the three kinds of market action that the Five Star system seeks to trade, plus the special case of the vacuum crash.

Chapter 24 - Some final advice.

---

[*] Homewood, Illinois: Business One Irwin, 1992.

Chapter 2

The Four-Price Line Chart

Two of the three kinds of market action which the Five Star system trades involve trading in the direction of an established bull or bear trend. But how do you know when you have a trend? In practice, one trader's correction in an assumed trend can be another trader's new trend. Put another way, there are trends within trends as there may be wheels within wheels.

Defining Bull, Bear and Sideways Trends

The *weekly* chart provides the basis for defining market trends. Generally, the weekly continuation chart does the job satisfactorily. However, when there are contract changeovers, especially ones involving major differences from one contract to the next as can occur in the agriculturals, the weekly chart for individual contracts serves better.

A bull trend should have a pattern of higher highs and higher lows on the weekly chart.

A bear trend should have a pattern of lower highs and lower lows.

A sideways, trading range or erratic trend has highs and lows occurring irregularly. Sometimes an upward or downward trending market has erratic highs or lows but the best markets to trade seldom violate a regular zigzag pattern until there is a major trend change.

W and M Formations

W and M formations are chart patterns that occur when a market is changing direction. They may be expected to mark the start of a zigzag in a new direction and, therefore, the start of a new trend.

A new bull market normally starts with a W in which the second low is ideally higher than the first one and the second high is higher than the preceding one. When the second low is marginally below the first one, assume a valid W after price exceeds the previous high. (Some technicians describe this formation as being a V-bottom.)

A bear market normally starts with an M in which there is a lower second high and a lower second low. As with a W, it can be reasonable to designate a valid M, despite a marginally higher second high, after the previous low is exceeded.

The concept of W and M formations is applicable to all price charts (weekly, daily, etc.) and also to the patterns that computer-based technical indicators generally make at tops and bottoms.

Sometimes price patterns trace out rather complex W or M formations, making smaller W or M patterns within the larger formation. The more cleanly a W or M pattern is formed, the stronger and better defined the ensuing trend is generally apt to be.

Under optimum circumstances, technical indicators all point in the direction of the assumed trend and also have a pattern of higher highs and higher lows in a bull market and vice versa in a bear market. Negative divergence occurs when the technical indicators and price do not go in the same direction. It is a warning that price may be about to reverse as well.

Recognizing Trends in Practice

The theoretical definitions of bull, bear and sideways trends sound obvious and simple to implement in practice. Unfortunately, in the world of real-time futures trading that is often not the case.

Consider, for example, the July 1991 move to a lower low in the Canadian Dollar (Chart 2.1). Did this move signify the end of the uptrend and the start of a new bear market? Or did the higher low and higher high in February and March 1993 indicate the start of a new bull market?

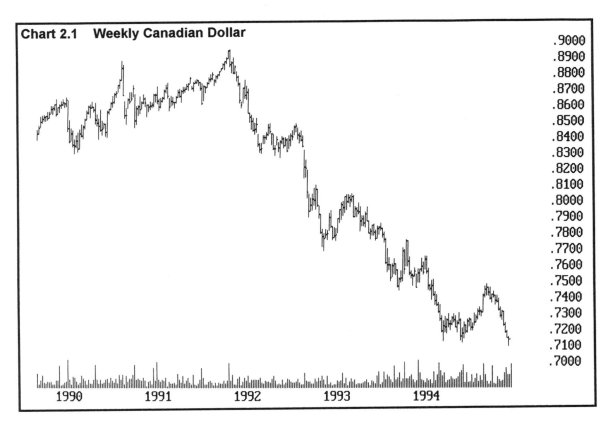

Chart 2.1 Weekly Canadian Dollar

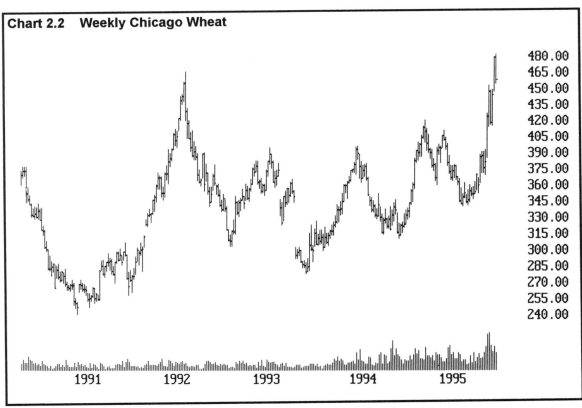

Chart 2.2 Weekly Chicago Wheat

The weekly chart for Wheat shows another aspect of the problem of designating a trend (Chart 2.2).   Between 1991 and 1994 Wheat turned sharply several times from a downtrend to an uptrend and then reversed.   An analytical approach based on waiting for Ms and Ws to form would have missed most of the big moves up and down in 1992 and 1994. (Note that the gaps in 1993 arise from contract changeovers, not market action.   Contract changeovers on the weekly continuation chart can appear to over- or understate price changes for specific contracts during the same period.)

The weekly chart for Gold shows essentially the opposite problem to that posed by Wheat (Chart 2.3). It has so many spikes and turns that it is difficult to decide which ones could be considered valid high or low points in hindsight, let alone when confronted with the need for a decision at the time. The 1991 and 1993 highs occurred with spikes or Vs and no topping process at all, let alone an identifiable M.

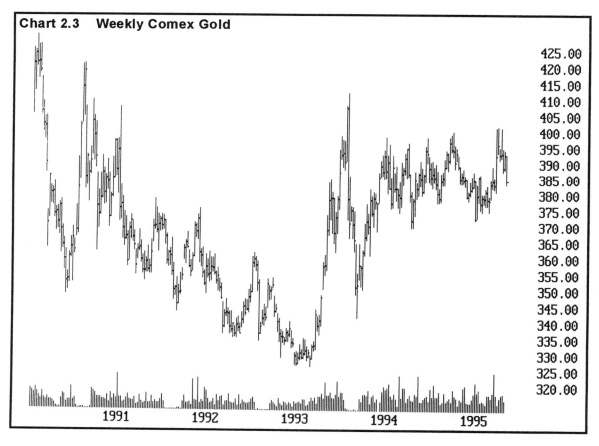

The weekly charts for the Canadian Dollar, Wheat and Gold show that determining a trend for the purpose of real-time trading can be very difficult in practice.   Since trading futures requires quick and efficient real-time decision-making, a better way of designating a trend is required.

The Four-Price Line Chart 11

Trends on the Weekly Four-Price Line Chart

The problem of designating a market trend does not lie with the concept of a bull trend having higher highs and higher lows, and vice versa for a bear trend. It can lie with finding a way to see through the clutter of a bar chart. To remedy this problem, we use a *weekly closing price* chart that is plotted as a continuous line. The price range for a given period is important but the closing price represents the result when all the ballots are counted.

For an initial assessment of market direction, we find that a weekly chart smoothed by averaging the four most recent closes is useful. It is a simple moving average of the last four weekly closes, termed "the weekly four-price line chart".

The smoothing effect of the four-price line has some tendency to show Ws as Vs. As noted earlier, price itself may sometimes also form more of a V than a W. Therefore, on the weekly chart:

A new bull market normally starts with a W: ideally, the second low is higher than the first one and the second high is higher than the preceding one. When the second low is somewhat below the previous low, assume a valid W when the four-price line or price (or both) exceeds the previous identifiable high.

The weekly four-price line chart for the Canadian Dollar leaves no doubt about its continuing bull market designation until the peak in November 1991 (Chart 2.4). In both 1992 and 1993 the four-price line rallied to the level of earlier highs but then turned and made double tops, indicating continuation of the major bear trend.

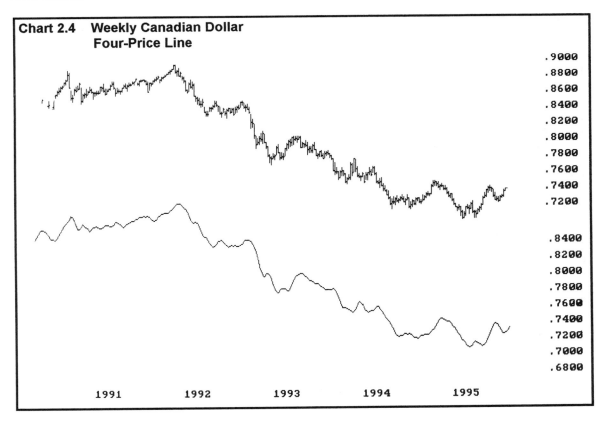

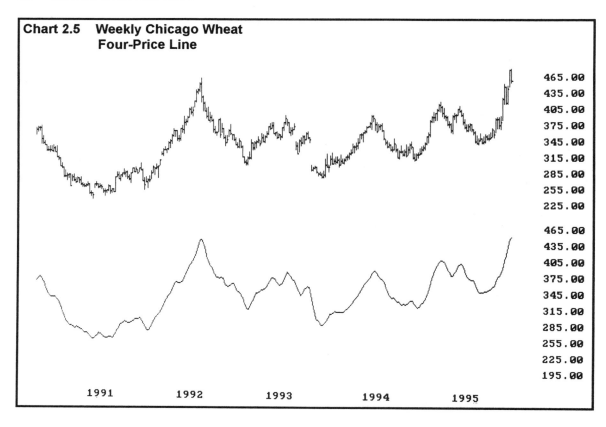

Chart 2.5   Weekly Chicago Wheat
             Four-Price Line

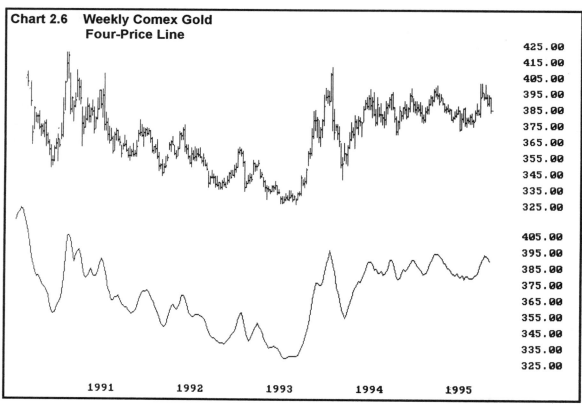

Chart 2.6   Weekly Comex Gold
             Four-Price Line

The weekly four-price line chart for Wheat shows many instances of how a market, once it turns, can immediately establish a new trend (Chart 2.5). Note also the Vs, rather than Ws, that occurred in the four-price line in mid-1992 and 1995. (The chart also shows the need to use stops in case there is no opportunity to mitigate a loss by waiting for price to retrace.)

Gold's weekly four-price line chart is quite erratic for much of the time, even during the period between the 1990 high and the 1993 low (Chart 2.6). This is a prime example of a market that requires other indicators to be used in conjunction with the four-price line. During 1994 and 1995, the four-price line showed clearly that Gold was in a sideways market that was unattractive to trade.

Testing Four-Price Line Signals on the Weekly Chart

As well as showing the trend of markets, the four-price line also delivers valuable market signals. When the four-price line changes direction, the probabilities favor continuation in the new direction for long enough to use it as a trading signal in both bull and bear markets.

We tested this indicator by itself on the weekly Gold chart to determine its usefulness. Although simulations are normally done on daily charts, we used the weekly chart because of the importance we attach to it and because of the long period that it covers. We want to stress that, in practice, no single indicator identifies trades with sufficient reliability to use on its own. However, any indicator that can deliver more than about 40 per cent profitable signals by itself is likely to be valuable, especially if profits significantly exceed losses.

We identified 72 turns on the Gold weekly four-price line between December 1992 and December 1994. Using only a turn to identify trends, we tested it by:

1. trading in the direction of the first turn;

2. on every subsequent turn, no matter how small, liquidating the current trade and initiating a new one in the opposite direction; and

3. using $12 ordinary stops from the initial entry and moving them by trailing to the next most favorable closing price, when there was one.

The hypothetical results, excluding commissions and slippage, and counting breakevens as losers, were:

15 Profits	(42%)	$12,650	Average Profit	$843
21 Losses	(58%)	7,470	Average Loss	$356
36 Trades		$ 5,180	Average Trade	$144

Given that profits exceeded losses by 69 per cent in this first test, we next tested the four-price line by:

1. buying only when a second turn occurred, forming a potential W, and thereby buying into an assumed bull market;

2.   selling only when a potential M occurred and thereby selling into an assumed bear market; and

3.   liquidating on an adverse turn.

The hypothetical results, using the same stops as in the first test, excluding commissions and slippage, and counting breakevens and losers, were:

8 Profits	(57%)	$7,860	Average Profit	$982
6 Losses	(43%)	1,990	Average Loss	$332
14 Trades		$5,870	Average Trade	$419

Waiting for an M to form on the weekly Gold chart missed one big move during the period examined, the big trade off the August 1993 high. Further examination of tops in many markets found that waiting for Ms to form at potential major market tops can result in missing too many of the biggest trades. Market tops often occur with a single turn on the weekly four-price line chart but market bottoms seldom do.

Given this finding, we next tested the question: What are the results of buying only on a double turn at the bottom (a W formation) but selling on a single turn at the top?

The hypothetical results for Gold, using the same stop and other conditions as in the previous two tests, were:

11 Profits	(52%)	$9,940	Average Profit	$904
10 Losses	(48%)	3,990	Average Loss	$399
21 Trades		$5,950	Average Trade	$283

This test produced results between those for random application of signals and application only with an M or a W. The results were clearly good enough to build on by introducing other indicators to filter in the potential big winners and to filter out ones having a low probability of success.

Wheat shows how major tops can occur with a single turn in the four-price line while bottoms generally require basing action before you can assume a new bull trend (Chart 2.5). Although the identification of a valid W at market bottoms is an important factor when looking for trades, the system does not rely on this indicator alone, or on any other single indicator to identify trades.

Four-Price Line Signals on the Daily Chart

We use the weekly chart to provide the basis for defining market trends, and for identifying which markets to trade and which to avoid. Once a market is identified as a potential trade, we use the daily chart to determine when to enter and to exit.

The four-price line on the daily chart does not have to form a W in order to enter a long position in a bull market. *Although a W is preferable, the four-price line only requires a turn in the direction of the intended trade for a valid signal.* A market can be deeply oversold as a result of a retracement, with a downward zigzag by the four-price line, without negating a bull market designation on the weekly chart. The deeply oversold condition may provide a prime opportunity for an entry when the four-price line turns up again.

The June 1994 Canadian Dollar chart is shown with the bar chart on top and the four-price line chart below (Chart 2.7). For illustrative purposes, we have used an adverse turn as an exit signal, although in practice we have a range of exit criteria (discussed in Chapter 19).

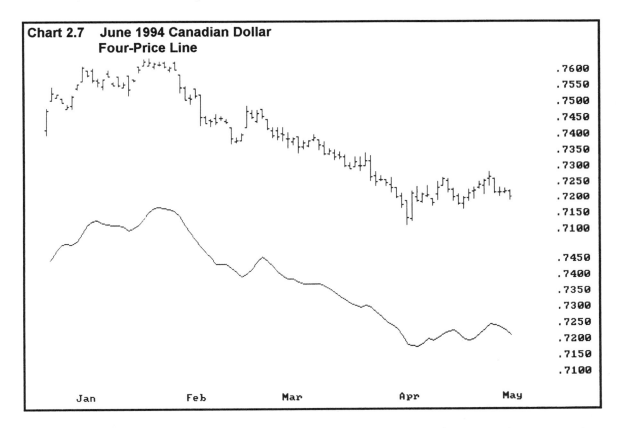

Chart 2.7 June 1994 Canadian Dollar Four-Price Line

The weekly Canadian Dollar four-price line chart delivered a sell signal with a downward turn on Friday, January 28 (Chart 2.4). Price action earlier in the week had suggested the possibility of a weekly downturn occurring. The four-price line on the daily chart turned down at .7605 on January 25 and this sell signal remained in force until an adverse turn up on February 17, at .7468, delivered an exit signal.

A signal to re-enter the short side occurred with the next turn down on February 24, at .7416. A tiny turn up on March 9 and 10 might have been ignored. A slightly larger turn up on March 23 delivered an exit signal (though not confirmed by other exit indicators discussed later), with liquidation at .7317. The final sell signal occurred on March 24, at .7267, with liquidation on April 7, at .7208.

The result was a total of three profitable trades, no losses and a gain of $2,950 before commissions and slippage.

The four-price line delivers relatively few signals. As the weekly Wheat chart shows (Chart 2.5), it may make only one turn at the start of a new trend and another one at the end of the trend—which actually signals the start of a new and opposite trend. This paucity of signals isn't important as we have other indicators for fine-tuning entries and exits.

The major use of the four-price line is to determine the trend. Therefore, it should point in the direction of an intended trade on the weekly chart and ideally, also on the daily chart. In addition, for bull trends it should show a W formation, as defined on page 11, and shown on page 8, in order to qualify as a valid signal on the weekly chart. For the daily chart, a simple upturn at lows is sufficient to qualify as a valid signal.

In the next chapter, we discuss an indicator that is similar but delivers many signals.

Chapter 3

The Single-Price Line Chart

The single-price line chart is exactly what it says, a simple line chart based on closing prices.* We use it to help qualify a market to trade on the weekly chart and to enter trades and liquidate them on the daily chart. The four-price line chart shows a broader or smoothed picture. The single-price line chart provides zigs and zags that can represent timely trading signals.

The difference between the four-price line and the single-price line may be compared with the tides of the sea. The four-price line shows the way the sea is running, while the single-price line comprises the erratic little waves that may run with or counter to the main flow.

We assume that under normal circumstances an adverse turn by the single-price line will be short lived when it moves against the direction of the four-price line and that it will turn back in the direction of the main wave or trend. The single-price line seldom maintains a completely regular zigzag pattern without violating previous lows in a rising market or previous highs in a declining market. But when it is making a regular zigzag pattern, the probabilities favor continuation of the trend.

Using the Weekly Single-Price Line Chart

1.   When the single-price line turns on the weekly chart, use it as a buy or sell indicator, as appropriate.

The importance of the single-price line as an indicator is particularly clear on the weekly chart for Wheat (Chart 3.1a). Wheat shows five major moves of more than 50 cents, including two of about $1, without an intervening turn on the four-price line (Chart 3.1b). Whenever the single-price line turned against the direction of the market, there was a prime opportunity to prepare for an entry when the weekly single-price line turned up again (using the daily chart to do so). Such

---

* Some software will automatically generate line charts based on closing prices. For software without this feature, the equivalent chart can be generated by setting the simple moving average at 1.

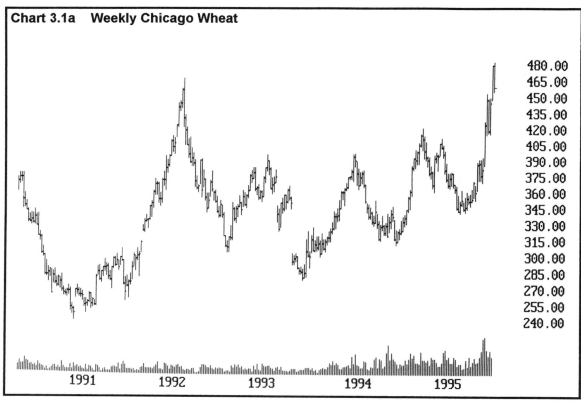

Chart 3.1a   Weekly Chicago Wheat

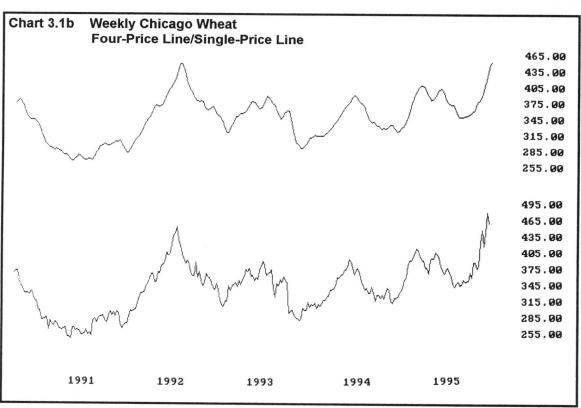

Chart 3.1b   Weekly Chicago Wheat
Four-Price Line/Single-Price Line

action suggests the end of a short-term correction. Except for the powerful move up in 1994, the single price-line on the weekly chart shows numerous confirming turns in the direction of major trends.

2. The most favorable moment for entering new *short* positions is when the single-price line turns down and the four-price line also points down, either concurrently or earlier. The reverse applies to entering new long positions.

    If the four-price line turns after the single-price line, this may be acceptable, depending on how the other indicators are acting. But it is not the preferred sequence. If the single-price line has already traveled far, it may be ready for a retracement.

3. For exits, the signals are the opposite of those for entry. The single-price line is usually the first of the indicators to turn against a trade. The four-price line may join it sooner or later, along with other indicators, to produce a signal to liquidate a trade.

On the basis of the four-price line, there was no reason to suspect that a turn at the November 1991 high might be the start of a new bear market in the Canadian Dollar. But one sign came from the single-price line, which began a very regular downward zigzag after the four-price line turned down, making a series of descending highs and lows (Chart 3.2b).

Between November 1991 and April 1994, there were several prime occasions when the Canadian Dollar renewed its qualification as a market to trade on the short side, with the four-price line and the single-price line both turning down more or less simultaneously at market crests. There were also many times when a downward turn in the single-price line resulted in a supplementary qualification of this as a market to trade.

Using the Daily Single-Price Line Chart

The June 1994 Canadian Dollar chart illustrates a principle discussed for the weekly charts: turns by the single-price line in the direction of the main trend have a high probability of following through when the four-price line is also pointing in the direction of the main trend (Chart 3.3b). When the turn occurs after a price correction lasting several days and the overall trend is strong, the probabilities are particularly favorable for a new entry. Note, in particular, the corrections in February and March that lasted for several days, followed by resumption of the downtrend with renewed vigor.

As on the weekly chart, single-price signals that occur when a four-price signal is not in force have a lower probability of following through. The action during much of May in the Canadian Dollar illustrates this principle.

The single-price line gives a relatively large number of signals compared with other indicators. Consequently, it often serves as a pivotal indicator when making trading decisions.

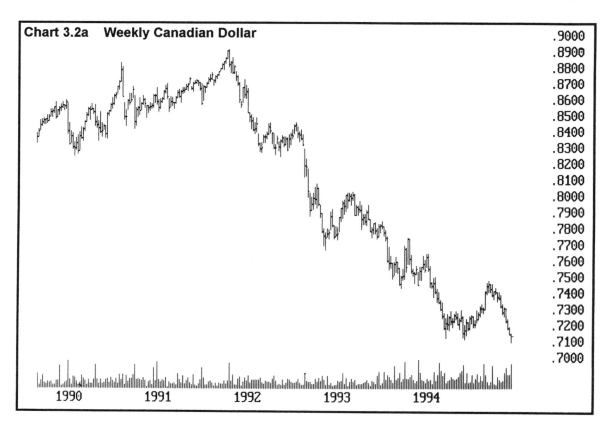

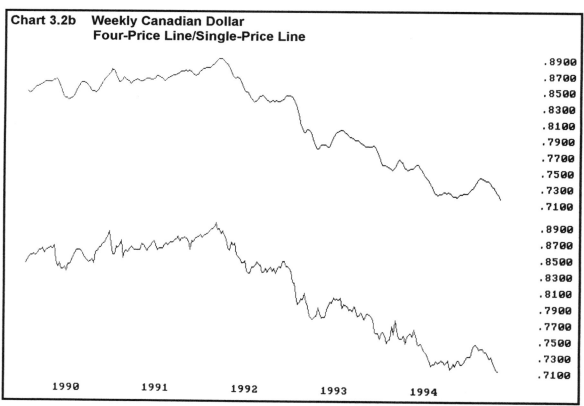

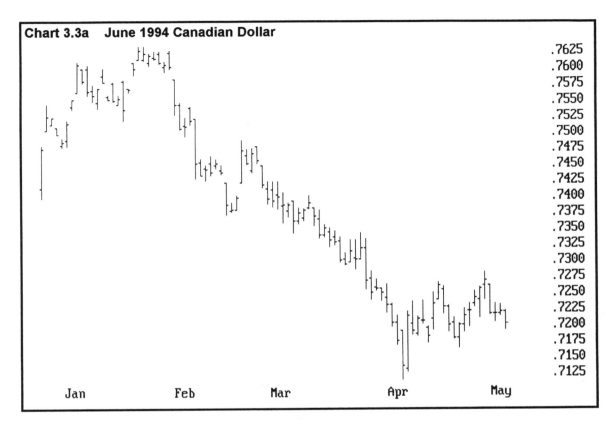

Chart 3.3a   June 1994 Canadian Dollar

.7625
.7600
.7575
.7550
.7525
.7500
.7475
.7450
.7425
.7400
.7375
.7350
.7325
.7300
.7275
.7250
.7225
.7200
.7175
.7150
.7125

Jan   Feb   Mar   Apr   May

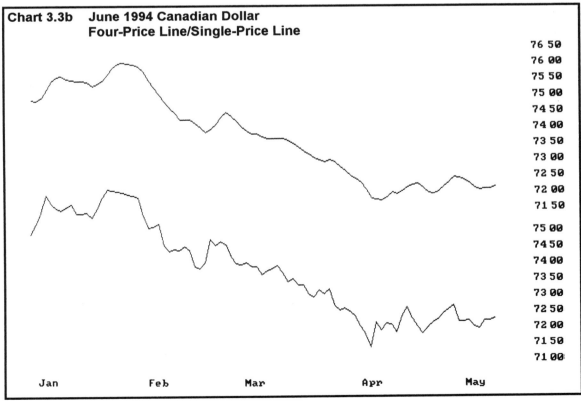

Chart 3.3b   June 1994 Canadian Dollar
Four-Price Line/Single-Price Line

76 50
76 00
75 50
75 00
74 50
74 00
73 50
73 00
72 50
72 00
71 50

75 00
74 50
74 00
73 50
73 00
72 50
72 00
71 50
71 00

Jan   Feb   Mar   Apr   May

Chapter 4

Moving Average Convergence/Divergence (MACD)

The moving average convergence/divergence (MACD) technical indicator is important for confirming trend changes and indicating the likely ability of a trend to continue. It therefore serves a combined function of showing direction and momentum. The Five Star system uses both functions of MACD to deliver signals.

MACD is a combination of three exponentially smoothed moving averages that are expressed as two lines. The faster line is an oscillator constructed by subtracting a shorter moving average from a longer one. The shorter moving average is constantly converging towards and diverging away from the longer one; hence the name. The slower line, generally (if misleadingly for our purposes) known as the signal line, is produced from an exponential moving average of the oscillator. We normally ignore the horizontal zero base line.

Setting for MACD

The setting for MACD that we use is: .15, .075, .20 or 12, 26, 9.

Both settings produce almost identical results. The first one expresses exponential values while the second set shows the actual duration for each of the three moving averages. Some software will accept only one format for these values.

The settings are in standard use and we have not been able to improve on them. You may encounter a second setting in some texts: 8, 17, 9. This setting was originally developed to deliver buy signals while the one we use was for sell signals and is somewhat slower acting. Because we use MACD in conjunction with other indicators, we find that our (slower) setting works well for both buying and selling.

Using MACD: Trend

Some of our uses of MACD are different from common practice. We use MACD to help determine the trend of markets in the following ways.

1.   On the weekly chart, MACD generally signals an impending change in market trend when it forms a double bottom or a double top, or when it makes a W or an M formation.

The weekly Canadian Dollar chart shows double tops in MACD in August 1990 and November 1991 (Chart 4.1). The second high in MACD was somewhat lower than the first one, although the price was higher. This bearish divergence suggested the possibility that price might turn down from the second high.

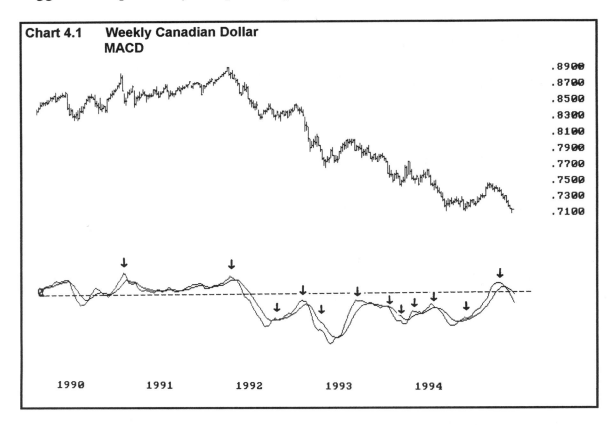

Chart 4.1   Weekly Canadian Dollar
MACD

2.   On the weekly chart, MACD confirms a trend when the fast line crosses the slow one, provided that:

a)   both lines trend in the same direction as price; and

b)   both lines maintain a roughly equal distance from each other.

3.   On both the weekly and daily charts, MACD gives a buy signal when the fast line turns up and a sell signal when it turns down. This indicator delivers signals on the same basis as the four- and single-price lines.

Of all the indicators that we use, MACD can be the slowest to react to market action. Therefore, it often delivers signals one or two price bars later than other indicators. It can also maintain an earlier signal in force while sufficient other indicators turn against a trade to dictate liquidation for a retracement. It is a sign of underlying strength in a trend when a MACD signal remains in force throughout a market retracement.

MACD turned down on the weekly Canadian Dollar chart in November 1991 (Chart 4.1). The new bear market was confirmed when the fast line crossed the slow one four weeks after the initial downturn. MACD's two lines both continued down for over four months, as price went from .8803 to .8383.

MACD turned up in March 1992 but delivered a new sell signal five weeks later, which was negated two weeks after that. No further sell signals occurred until the market crested three months later and the fast oscillator turned down with price at .8315.

Other signals qualifying the Canadian Dollar as a market to sell short are marked on the chart. From May to August 1993 the slow and fast lines converged into almost a single line with a gentle downward incline. With price also working lower in a regular pattern of lower highs and lower lows, it was possible to sit back and let short positions ride.

In October 1993 MACD turned up after making a higher low than in late 1992, thereby suggesting that the major trend might have changed. However, by early 1994 price action suggested that the major bear trend remained in force. Subsequent action provides a good example of how MACD and price can diverge. The reason for it is discussed in the next section on momentum.

The weekly Wheat chart shows MACD at its best for quickly identifying major changes in market trend (Chart 4.2). Once turned, MACD kept its signals in force almost without interruption throughout most of the major moves.

Similarly, MACD indicated all the major turns on the weekly Gold chart, with the rounding most pronounced prior to the major move up in 1993 (Chart 4.3).

We analysed the signals from the MACD fast line on the weekly Gold chart and the signals from the four-price line chart for the same period (Chart 2.6 in Chapter 2). The results were so similar that it is more useful to point out the differences rather than the similarities.

When the four-price line turned down in June 1993, MACD kept on going up, thereby failing to qualify Gold as a market to sell short and averting a losing trade. When the eventual top came, both indicators coincided in confirming it. With the steady downtrend in MACD during 1994, any possibility of trading the long side of Gold, based on its four-price line action, should have been resolved by MACD in favor of not buying it.

4. On the daily chart, MACD defines a steadily moving market, and generally also a rapidly moving market, when the chart pattern for the fast line:

   a) forms a regular W or M and then proceeds to zigzag steadily higher (after a W formation) or lower (after an M formation); or

   b) trends steadily above the slow line in a bull market or below it in a bear market.

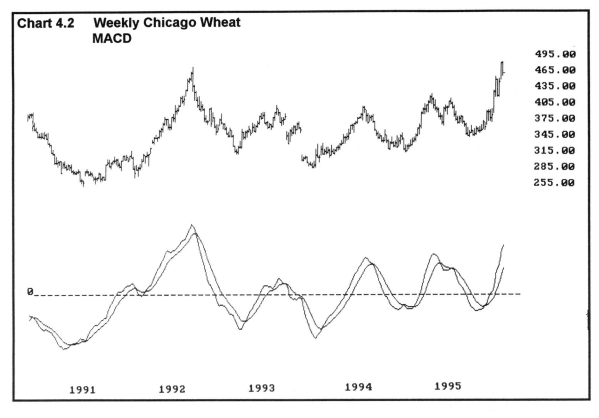

Chart 4.2   Weekly Chicago Wheat
MACD

495.00
465.00
435.00
405.00
375.00
345.00
315.00
285.00
255.00

0

1991   1992   1993   1994   1995

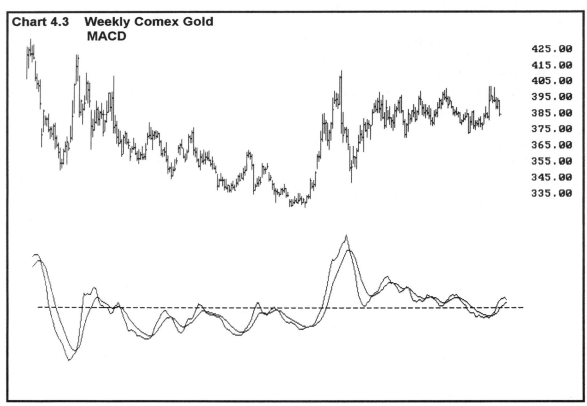

Chart 4.3   Weekly Comex Gold
MACD

425.00
415.00
405.00
395.00
385.00
375.00
365.00
355.00
345.00
335.00

In some markets, more of a position-trading approach is appropriate because price is moving steadily in the direction of the trend, with only small retracements. When MACD is steadily trending, the balance of decision-making can be tipped slightly toward staying in a trade rather than liquidating when a weak or ambiguous exit signal occurs. Normally, we pull the trigger faster for an exit than an entry. However, just as there are stronger and weaker entry signals, so there can be variations in the strength of exit signals. A trending MACD provides the one situation when it may be appropriate to let a trade run.

The June 1994 Canadian Dollar chart shows the MACD fast line confirming a downward zigzag with its downturn on February 24 (Chart 4.4). Apart from its standard use as a signal in its own right, this downturn confirmed the probability that the bear market would continue a further worthwhile distance. Until the low at the beginning of April, the MACD fast line worked steadily lower, remaining just below the slow line and thereby suggesting that price could also work steadily lower.

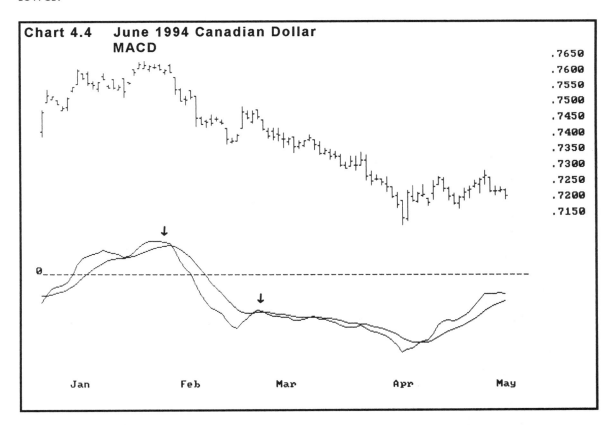

Using MACD: Momentum

We also use MACD, *on both the weekly and daily charts*, to help determine the momentum of markets and thus, by extension, their potential to change direction.

1.   MACD often shows underlying shifts in momentum, particularly on the weekly chart, long before price action responds with a change in the trend. Therefore, when weekly MACD turns in the opposite direction to price, it does not mean that trades against MACD's new direction should be avoided.

   Trading decisions are based on the net result of the signals from many indicators and there is almost never a complete absence of conflicts. Trades are particularly favorable when MACD is confirming and they should be regarded with caution, but by no means be embargoed, when MACD is in conflict.

The weekly Canadian Dollar chart provides a good example of how MACD acts when the initial forceful momentum of a new trend starts slowing, even though the major trend remains quite steadily in force (Chart 4.1).

The Canadian Dollar moved in 13 months from a high of .8906 in November 1991 to a low of .7663 in December 1992, for a total move of 1,243 points. The market subsequently moved from a retracement high of .8017 in late March 1993 to the apparent final bear market low at .6983 in January 1995, for a total move of 1,034 points in 27 months. In round numbers, the second stage of the bear market lasted twice as long as the first but price declined by only 83 percent of its decline in the first stage.

While the Canadian Dollar remained in a major bear market throughout the period, price action during the final 27 months was characterised by substantially more rallies and consolidations than accompanied the initial phase. MACD reflected this difference in momentum on the weekly chart by reaching its low point in December 1992. Note that both MACD and price action produced a W formation at the bear market bottom in early 1995.

The weekly Wheat chart similarly shows momentum shifting upward over a period of almost a year in 1991-92, while price went essentially sideways with an upward bias, until the upside breakout (Chart 4.2). Despite the fact that MACD had come so far off the bottom, it was still only around the level of the zero base line when it gave the significant buy signal that marked the start of the major move up from mid-1991.

2.   The fast line normally moves away from the slow one as momentum increases. There is often a bulge by the fast line away from the slow one at major tops or bottoms, or at points from which a major retracement is likely to occur. When there is a bulge on the *weekly* chart after a market has made an extended move, there is a high probability of a major trend change.

The weekly and daily charts for the Canadian Dollar and the weekly Wheat and Gold charts all show clearly how the fast line pulls away from the slow line as momentum increases and then bulges as price makes a final stretch to significant highs or lows (Charts 4.1 to 4.4).

Entries and Exits on the Daily Chart

The Five Star system uses MACD to deliver signals for entering and liquidating trades when the fast line turns, in the same way that the four-price line and the single-price line are used.

The June 1994 Canadian Dollar chart shows a good example of why a market has to be qualified first on the weekly chart prior to entering trades on the basis of the daily chart (Chart 4.4). MACD delivered a clear signal to enter a short position when it turned down on January 11. However, the weekly chart did not meet the requirements to qualify the Canadian Dollar as ready to sell short (Chart 4.1), and price went almost a cent higher.

On January 25, MACD turned down again and price action also suggested a high probability of a top. MACD's sell signal on the daily chart remained in force from that day. However, MACD turned down on the weekly chart only as a result of the next week's price action, thereby illustrating the need to have a variety of indicators on which to base trading decisions.

MACD turned up, negating the short sale, when price gapped up on February 17 and closed higher. This move turned out to be a short-term retracement. MACD gave a new sell signal on February 24 on a close at .7416. This was below the exit price but it identified an entry for a further major move down, until the big upside reversal on April 5, which closed at .7212. (In practice, other indicators confirmed re-entry on February 23 at .7453. Although MACD's signal was one day later in this instance, our coordination of several indicators means that we achieve the best available compromises over time.)

The June 1994 Canadian Dollar chart shows why it is necessary to use the fast line for signals when it turns, rather than waiting for crossovers. The crossover to the upside in December 1993 warned that a more significant retracement might be starting but it occurred too late for a satisfactory exit signal. In January 1994 the first bulge and subsequent convergence of the fast line back toward the slow line suggested the possibility of a top but, as already mentioned, the weekly chart did not give a short sale signal. The crossover at the top confirmed the validity of a short position but it occurred only after the market had come significantly off the top. Once crossed, the probabilities suggested by this indicator continued to be favorable for entering short positions until the upturn on April 5.

MACD, like the four-price line, is very useful for evaluating the potential for market turns. It needs to be used, however, in conjunction with an overbought/oversold indicator when attempting to differentiate between those turns that are routine and those that may involve major trend changes. Stochastics, discussed in Chapter 7, provide the cross reference most useful for making this distinction.

Chapter 5

Price Rules

This chapter takes a break from discussing computer-generated technical indicators to look directly at price formations, because this information will be used in the following chapters.

Price formations are patterns of price movements and closes that we look for on the weekly, daily and 60-minute charts. We have identified eight important price formations and have synthesized them into Five Star "price rules". (Don't despair: these rules should be easy to learn and, with practice, you will come to recognize them almost automatically.)

On the weekly charts, we use price rules, together with other indicators, for pattern recognition; that is, to predict market turning points and to confirm the direction of the market. Completion of a price rule on the weekly chart *qualifies* a market to trade when other indicators come together in sufficient number.

On the daily charts, we normally use price rules to pull the trigger *to enter or exit* a trade, provided that there are enough other confirming indicators, including an emerging or existing price rule on the weekly chart. For example, if a weekly reversal appears to be developing, based on the price action on Monday and Tuesday, and a *daily* price rule occurs on Tuesday, you don't have to wait until the close on Friday before trading. For exits, completion of a price rule signal to trade in the opposite direction is strongly preferred but not essential. When there is no price rule signal, base the exit decision on the quality of the signals confirming liquidation plus the overall picture, including the sentiment and "other" indicators (summarised in Chapter 18).

Principles and Conditions

Before describing the price rules, you may find it useful to know the principles on which they are based.

1. A daily or weekly close at the extremity of a bar's range suggests that the market is likely to continue in the direction of the strong close, provided that there are several consecutive strong closes in the same direction.

2.   A market is likely to continue in the direction in which it gaps, particularly when it closes at the extremity of the range in the direction of the gapping.

3.   A market is likely to continue in the direction of a reversal bar, provided that there is a strong close in the direction of the reversal.

All the price rules are subject to the following conditions:

1.   A trading formation is completed only when the *final bar* has a close in the top or bottom 25 percent of the bar's range, as appropriate.

2.   Because of the requirement that price should close in the top or bottom 25 percent of the range to complete a signal, formations may take longer to complete than the minimum time specified by the rules. Thus, you might not have a valid entry in accordance with Rule 1 until the fourth or even fifth bar.

3.   When price closes in the middle of the range, the result is regarded as neutral and is given the same designation as the previous bar.

4.   When an emerging pattern is violated, you must start counting again at the beginning of the potential price formation.

5.   When a price rule signal is given (and other indicators confirm a trade), enter the trade on that day's close or the next day's open. Do not chase entries unless there is a reversal bar with the trend (a new rule 6 signal) or powerful market action such as a breakout with a gap. The risk of a retracement usually increases as the market moves away from a price rule signal.

Price Rule 1: Three-Bar Closes

A buy signal occurs on completion of three consecutive bars in which price closes in the upper half of the range.

A sell signal occurs on completion of three consecutive bars in which price closes in the lower half of the range.

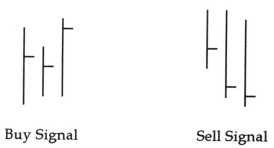

Buy Signal   Sell Signal

Price Rule 2: Reversals

Shorten the proving time for the trading formation from three bars to two when either of the two bars is a reversal: closing price, key or high/low reversal.

A *closing price upside reversal* occurs when price has exceeded the previous bar's low and closes at the same price as the previous bar, or higher. A *downside reversal* occurs when price has exceeded the high of the previous bar and closes at the same price as the previous bar, or lower.

A *key reversal* occurs when price initially makes a significant new low or high in the direction of the trend but then reverses sharply and closes beyond the previous high or low. These reversals often occur on climactic volume and signal a continuation in the direction of the close. We also use this term for outside days during the course of a move regardless of the opening price.

A *high/low reversal* occurs when price closes at or near one extremity one day and at or near the other extremity the next day. High/low reversals are not always completely clear, especially when there is gapping involved, but the close of the second bar should be in the top or bottom 25 per cent of the bar's range, as appropriate and, ideally, at its extremity.

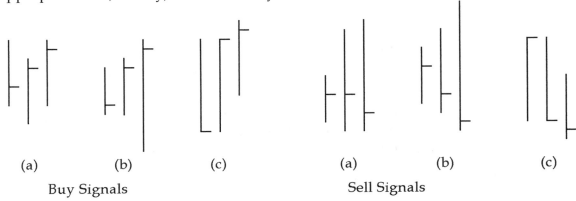

(a)	(b)	(c)		(a)	(b)	(c)
	Buy Signals				Sell Signals	

(a) closing price reversal   (b) key reversal   (c) high/low reversal

Price Rule 3: Gaps

A gap occurs when there is a blank space between one bar and the next one, or when price draws away from the close of the previous bar and fails to fill the gap on a closing basis.

Shorten the proving time from three bars to two when a gap occurs.

Buy Signals   Sell Signals

Price Rule 4: Islands

An island occurs when there is a blank space on the chart as a result of price first gapping up and then down, or vice versa. An island also occurs when price gaps away from a close first in one direction and then in the other, even if the ranges of two or more bars overlap.

Shorten the proving time to one bar when an island occurs.

Buy Signal   Sell Signal

It is not necessary for closing price(s) within an island to be in the top or bottom of the range.

An island may consist of one bar or many. However, the more time taken to form an island and the more symmetrical the gapping, the more likely that there is an important turning point. This is because islands often indicate absolute exhaustion of the previous trend. They are therefore a particularly reliable indicator of the end of an established trend in one direction and the beginning of a move in the opposite direction.

Price Rule 5a: Lindahl Buy

a   b c d e

Buy Signal

Within *nine* calendar days (or weeks on the weekly chart) from the bar of the low for the formation:

1.   price must exceed the high of the bottom bar for the formation: (b) must take out the high of (a);

2.   price must then take out the low of the preceding bar: (d) must take out the low of (c); and

3.   to buy, price must take out the high of the preceding bar, and close above the preceding bar's close and the current bar's opening price (e).

This formation may be completed in as few as three calendar days or weeks, or as many as *nine*, depending on how many bars intervene that do not contribute to development of the formation.

Price Rule 5b: Lindahl Sell

a   b   c   d   e

Sell Signal

Within *eight* calendar days (or weeks on the weekly chart) from the bar of the high for the formation:

1.   price must exceed the low of the top bar for the formation: (b) must take out the low of (a);

2.   price must then take out the high of the preceding bar: (d) must take out the high of (c); and

3.   to sell, price must take out the low of the preceding bar, and close below the preceding bar's close and the current bar's opening price (e).

This formation may be completed in as few as three calendar days or weeks, or as many as *eight*, depending on how many bars intervene that do not contribute to development of the formation.

Price Rule 6: Trend Continuation

Shorten the proving time to one bar when there is a single reversal bar in the direction of an *established and unmistakable trend.*

Buy Signals   Sell Signals

It is psychologically difficult to chase a rapidly moving market. But this rule provides the mechanism for getting into a fast-moving market with a manageable stop loss and with a very high probability of making a good profit quickly. (The stop is just beyond the extremity of the price range on the entry day.)

This rule is also used to enter a trade on the assumption that a consolidation within a clearly established trend is ending.

Price Rule 7: Trend Reversals

Trade with the direction of a single, very big reversal bar when price has reached a major target level.

Buy Signal   Sell Signal

The most common use of this rule is when price retraces and reaches or comes close to moving averages that are pointing in the direction of an established trend. An additional, although rare, use of this rule occurs when price has reached a horizontal objective and there is a reversal of such unmistakable power that you can justify assuming that the market has completed a buying or selling climax. Even so, it is remarkable how often a market has to take another run at highs or lows. Therefore, the use of this rule for a contra-trend trade has a lower probability of success than most traders would normally consider acceptable.

Price Rule 8: Double Reversals

Enter a trade on completion of a second reversal bar in the same direction within a period of about five or six bars—whether closing price reversals, high/low reversals or a combination. Both reversal bars should close in the top or bottom 25 percent, as appropriate, of the bars' ranges.

Buy Signals   Sell Signals

As suggested by the name double reversal, this rule is a double trend continuation (Rule 6) or two reversals (Rule 2). Since double reversals occur often, are particularly reliable and can come in hybrid configurations (as illustrated), it is appropriate to recognize their importance with a separate rule.

Double reversals are often contained within Lindahl formations. The signal is much stronger if the second low is higher when buying, or if the second high is lower when selling—unless the second reversal is exceptionally powerful.

Illustrating the Price Rules

The price rules are shown on the chart for July 1994 Cotton (Chart 5.1, page 38). Actual execution of trades at the indicated points would depend on the signals from other indicators.

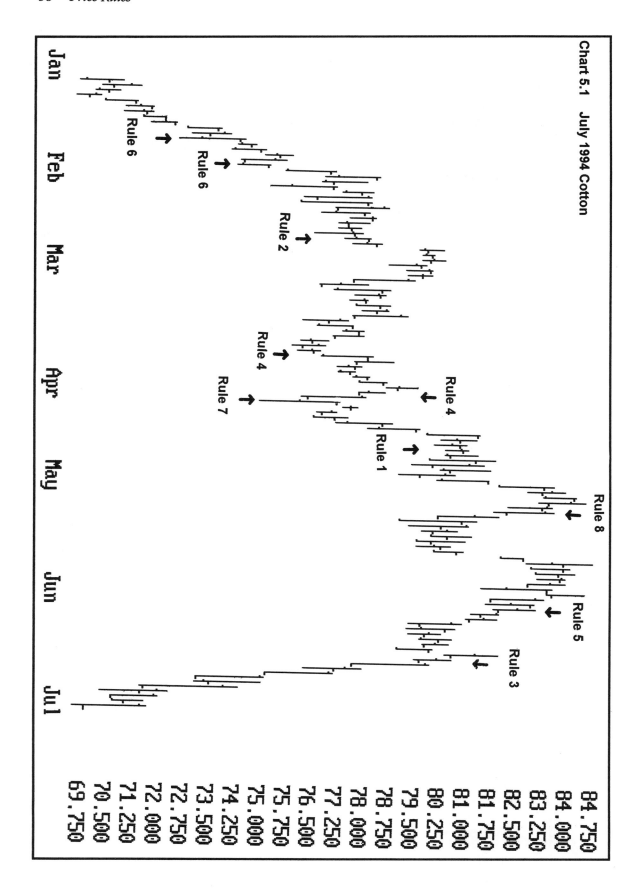

Chart 5.1   July 1994 Cotton

Chapter 6

Moving Averages

A moving average is a curved version of a trendline or a smoothed version of a trend. The Five Star system uses moving averages to confirm the direction of the trend, to deliver trading signals when they turn and to indicate potential support and resistance levels.

A crossover of one moving average by another one, or by price, is a signal for many traders to trade in the direction of the crossover. However, we find that crossovers are more likely to deliver losses than profits: they may simply be an expression of an overbought condition when crossing to the upside or of an oversold condition when crossing below.

Setting for Moving Averages

We use two *simple* moving averages, with settings of: 25, 40.

Simple moving averages are in more widespread use than weighted or exponential moving averages and we believe that they produce better results. The 25 and 40 settings are used by many traders; their effectiveness for potential support and resistance levels therefore tends to be self-fulfilling. The 40-week moving average corresponds very closely to the 200-day moving average, which is widely used by traders interested in identifying long-term changes in market direction.

Using Moving Averages

1. The 25- and 40-*week* moving averages generally indicate the direction of the major trend. On the weekly chart, the 25- and especially the 40-week moving averages can show the same direction for months, and sometimes years, without turning. Flat moving averages generally indicate a trading range market, which we try to avoid.

   While moving averages are excellent trend-following indicators, they are not useful for indicating how strong a market is and, thus, when it reaches an overbought or oversold level. Consequently, they do not show when a market may be subject to a retracement or a major trend change.

Our simple moving averages reflect, on an unweighted basis, price information over 25 and 40 periods. Therefore, like supertankers, it takes some time for them to reverse direction. Trend changes can occur suddenly and violently, particularly at tops, but they will not be reflected on the weekly moving averages until many weeks after the event. This is why we use stochastics, and the single- and four-price lines to identify major turns.

2.   Each of the 25- and 40-period moving averages delivers a buy or sell signal *when it turns*. A signal continues in force for as long as each moving average points in the same direction; that is, until it turns again.

3.   During price corrections, the moving averages should act as support or resistance levels, as appropriate, and contain price on a closing basis.

Note, though, one important difference between the use of this guideline on the weekly and daily charts. Price on the *weekly* chart should, ideally, not make more than one adverse close on the other side of the 40-week moving average. But on the *daily* chart, adverse closes may simply be an expression of a very overbought or oversold market, provided that price fluctuations are contained by the 40-week moving average on the weekly chart. The *weekly* chart shows the big picture for market direction. Therefore, an overbought or oversold *daily* chart within the boundaries of acceptable fluctuations on the *weekly* chart may provide a prime opportunity to buy low in a bull market or to sell high in a bear market.

The weekly Canadian Dollar chart shows a market in a major bear trend from November 1991 (Chart 6.1). The 25-week moving average first confirmed a major trend change the week of December 20, 1991, seven weeks after the weekly high close and after price had already fallen from .8898 to .8593 (basis the weekly close). The 40-week moving average confirmed the trend change five weeks later, on January 24, 1992. Other indicators signaled the probability of a major top well before the moving averages confirmed the trend change (as discussed in earlier chapters). But once the new bear trend was confirmed by the moving averages, it was reasonable to assume that there would be a succession of profitable trading opportunities on the sell side.

Price often extended far away from the moving averages and then retraced back toward them. When price and the moving averages converged, turns at or near the 40-week moving average led to continuation of the trend for almost three years, until the adverse close above it on September 16, 1994.

The June 1994 Canadian Dollar shows that price moved above the 25- and 40-day moving averages for almost a month in January (Chart 6.2). At the same time, price moved up near the 40-week moving average on the weekly chart but did not go through. Price then turned and went back down through the 25-week moving average the week of January 28, 1994. (Our other computer-based technical indicators also turned down that week, confirming the continuation of the bear trend.) As well, price moved down through the daily moving averages on January 28.

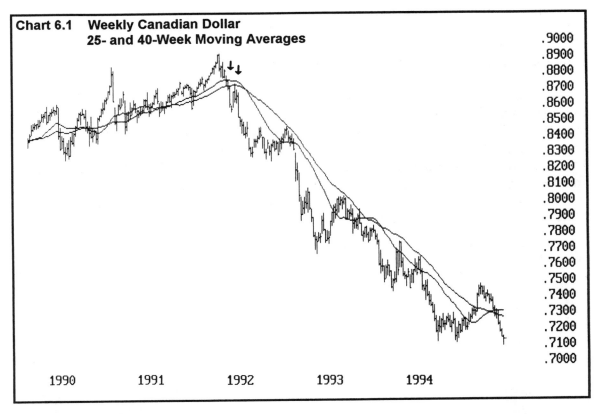

Chart 6.1 Weekly Canadian Dollar
25- and 40-Week Moving Averages

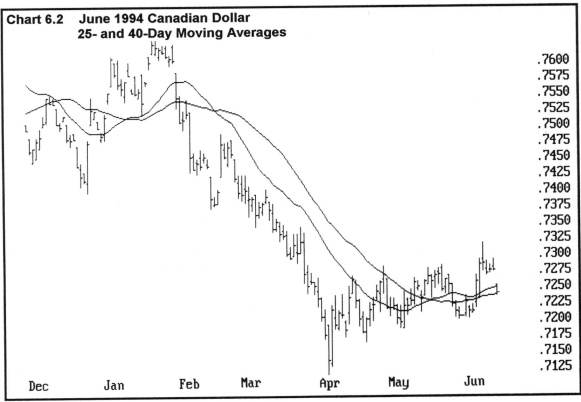

Chart 6.2 June 1994 Canadian Dollar
25- and 40-Day Moving Averages

In this instance, the market became very overbought in the short term, but remained within the confines of the long-term bear market on the weekly chart. Therefore, the conjunction of indicators giving new sell signals on January 28 provided a prime opportunity to enter new short positions.

Unlike the weekly Canadian Dollar chart, the weekly Gold chart shows a market in which price continually lunged across the moving averages between 1991 and 1993 (Chart 6.3). The moving averages were generally pointing sideways or strongly down but failed to provide resistance on rallies, despite the bear trend. Evidently many traders were expecting a new bull market and kept trying to buy it. In any case, Gold's price action in relation to the moving averages is similar to what we saw when discussing the four-price line and MACD: between 1991 and 1993 Gold was a source of few prime trades and was generally a market to avoid.

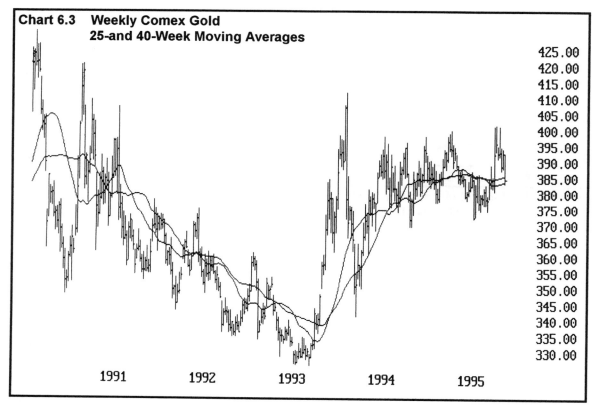

Chart 6.3   Weekly Comex Gold
25-and 40-Week Moving Averages

425.00
420.00
415.00
410.00
405.00
400.00
395.00
390.00
385.00
380.00
375.00
370.00
365.00
360.00
355.00
350.00
345.00
340.00
335.00
330.00

1991   1992   1993   1994   1995

From early 1994, the moving averages indicate a sideways trend in Gold. The December 1994 Gold chart shows price lunging above and below the moving averages, reflecting the trading range on the weekly chart (Chart 6.4). Thus, the moving averages on both the weekly and daily charts indicate that Gold did not offer any Five Star trades during 1994.

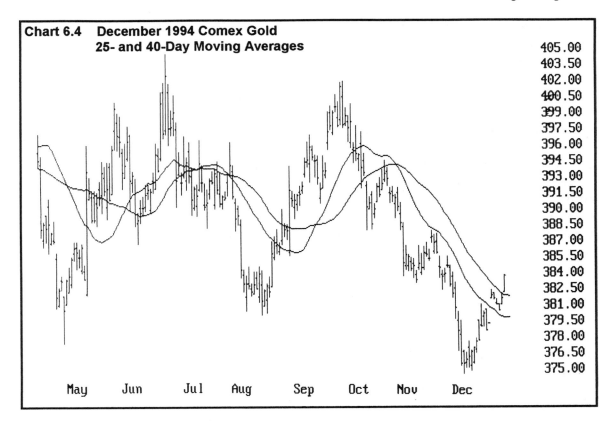

**Chart 6.4 December 1994 Comex Gold
25- and 40-Day Moving Averages**

4. A price rule signal (described in Chapter 5) that occurs at or near the 25- or 40-period moving average *after a retracement* has a high probability of following through. It shows that the retracement has most likely ended and applies to both the weekly and daily charts with considerable reliability.

A *weekly price reversal in the direction of the trend* (price rule 6) which occurs at or near either the 25- or 40-week moving average is one of the strongest signals of the trend continuing, provided that both moving averages point in the direction of the reversal. *But if this signal is preceded by more than one adverse close outside both moving averages within the last five bars, it should be regarded with suspicion.*

A weekly reversal at or near favorably inclining moving averages occurs relatively seldom. When it does, it almost invariably suggests that you should look for an entry and, if necessary, liquidate other trades in order to respond to this signal. The probability of a successful trade increases exponentially when there are second and third weekly reversals having higher highs, lows and closes in a bull market, and vice versa in a bear market.

A weekly reversal at or near either of the moving averages should not be confused with weekly reversals that occur when price has moved away from the averages. While such reversals may be valid signals of a market's ability to continue further, they inevitably occur when price is more vulnerable to a retracement than with reversals that occur at or near the moving averages.

There is no such thing as a "sure thing" in futures trading but a weekly reversal at or near trending moving averages comes as close as you're likely to come to finding it.

The weekly Canadian Dollar chart shows six closing price reversals and four high/low reversals in the direction of the trend that occurred at or near the moving averages during the bear market (Chart 6.1). Two of these were also price rule 5 Lindahl sell signals. Several of the closing price reversals occurred immediately before a significant continuation of the downtrend and none of the reversal bar highs were exceeded before the downtrend continued. Every short sale entered on completion of the six weekly downside reversals, including the two Lindahl sell signals, can therefore be assumed to be profitable. Of the four high/low reversals, three were profitable and one unprofitable, judged by the same criteria.

The weekly chart for Wheat also demonstrates both the rarity and the high success rate of price rule signals at the moving averages (Chart 6.5). Between August 1991 and June 1995 there were nine such signals when at least one of the moving averages pointed in the direction of the price signal. Seven were closing price reversals, one was a high/low reversal and one a three bar close signal. Eight of the nine signals could be judged profitable by our criteria, with the high/low reversal unsuccessful. Realistically, however, the closing price reversal for the week ended December 2, 1994, should be counted as a loser if reasonable stop placement is considered. The success rate was therefore seven out of nine.

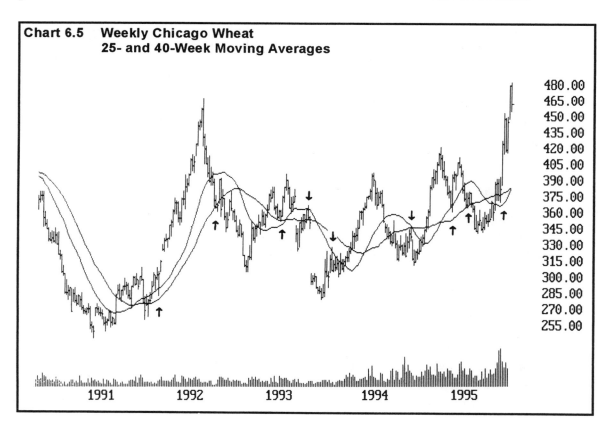

Chart 6.5   Weekly Chicago Wheat
25- and 40-Week Moving Averages

The September 1995 S&P 500 chart shows how the 25- and 40-day moving averages contained retracements during its big bull move (Chart 6.6). There were 11 buying opportunities when the market turned up at or near the moving averages in order to resume the advance. Given the power of the market, you could enter with reasonable confidence on the first day the market reversed or showed strength at the moving averages, on the basis of a price rule 6 trend continuation buy signal in a strongly trending market. A turn at the beginning of July, when price only came within 250 points of the 25-day moving average, is included in the total. Sometimes you must make a call as to what constitutes price being at or near the moving averages. A retracement that doesn't return to the moving averages shows a strong market if the turn is clear.

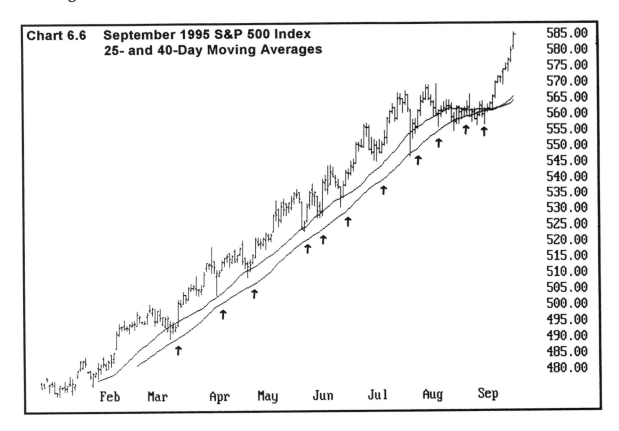

**Chart 6.6   September 1995 S&P 500 Index
25- and 40-Day Moving Averages**

During August, when the market was consolidating, three good reversal entry signals didn't work and resulted in small losses. But after the fourth signal, a powerful double reversal, the market surged up. The net result of the eleven entries was eight profits and three losses, with the huge profits almost burying the losses.

The concept of price turns at or near the moving averages works best when there has not been an adverse close within the last five bars on the weekly or daily chart, as applicable. Trade in the direction of a trend that is both established and shows that it can behave. This concept is unrelated to the dreaded moving average crossover theory of trading and is infinitely more reliable, since random crossovers are more likely to fail than to follow through.

5.   Some of the best trades occur when the 25- and 40-period moving averages show a convex rounding pattern. The general rule is that the longer such a pattern takes to develop, the more likely it is to follow through. A rounding pattern that takes several weeks or even months to develop on the weekly chart is virtually certain to show similar rounding on the daily chart.

The May 1995 Cotton chart provides an almost perfect example of a market rounding out at the bottom and slowly gathering speed in the early stages of what became a classic major bull market (Chart 6.7). This chart also shows how 25- and 40-period moving averages are unable to provide signals of price retracements.

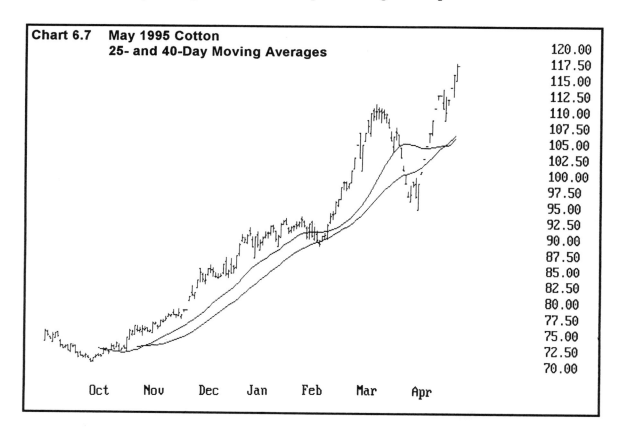

**Chart 6.7   May 1995 Cotton
25- and 40-Day Moving Averages**

Chapter 7

Stochastics

There are many ways to use stochastics. The Five Star system uses them in an unusual way because it focuses on the behavior of the fast stochastic line, %K, rather than its slow line, %D, and crossovers of the two lines.

%K performs two prime functions: to identify overbought and oversold markets, and thus the potential for both short-term and major tops and bottoms, and second, to deliver buy and sell signals when %K turns. For this second function, we use %K in much the same way as we use the single-price line for the delivery of immediate signals within a bigger picture.

Stochastics show the relationship between the most recent close and the high-low range for a chosen time period. They are similar to the Relative Strength Index (RSI). But because the RSI is based only on closing prices for a given period, it doesn't reflect the full range of price action. We want this information to be reflected in our core overbought/oversold indicator because we attribute particular importance to where price closes in relation to the range of a given bar.

Stochastics are useful for indicating overbought and oversold levels because, unlike MACD, they fluctuate on a scale between zero and 100. In sideways markets and in markets fluctuating within the identifiable confines of an uptrend or a downtrend, stochastics tend to swing back and forth between overbought and oversold levels.

Note, though, that stochastics can be an extremely deceptive indicator. They can quickly go to an overbought or oversold reading and stay there for a considerable time. It is therefore essential to consider them with other indicators.

Setting for Stochastics

The setting we use is for *slow* stochastics: 9, 3, 3S. Some software may not require the "S" to indicate that the setting is for slow rather than fast stochastics.

Slow stochastics at this setting are widely used. The setting expresses the following: %K is based on 9, the number of bars included in the calculations; %D is a 3-day moving average of %K, and the final 3 smoothes both %K and %D to produce the slow stochastics. (Fast stochastics, which lack the smoothing, are far more choppy.)

Using Stochastics

As with our other computer-based technical indicators, we examine %K first on the weekly chart and then on the daily chart. Note that %K has different parameters on the weekly and daily charts.

1. On the *weekly* chart, a market is overbought at a %K reading of 80 or higher, and oversold at 20 or lower.

    When %K is at 80 or above, look for the possibility of a major market downturn to be indicated by:

    a)   %K turning down and returning below 80, and/or by %K crossing %D (which may occur at the same time); and

    b)   other indicators turning down, notably the four-price line and MACD.

    By itself, a turn by %K at an overbought or oversold level is *only an alert* that the trend may change. An initial turn by %K can occur long before the trend changes and there may be numerous false signals that are not confirmed by other indicators such as the four-price line and MACD.

    The probability of a major top increases in proportion to the extent of the overbought condition of %K: a reading above 90, which is quite rare, normally indicates that a market top is at hand. When there has been a powerful bull market, the probability of a trend change also increases exponentially with the number of times %K turns back below 80 and with the number of times that it crosses %D.

2. When %K is at 20 or below on the weekly chart, apply the same principles in reverse, with one important difference. As noted in Chapter 2, the four-price line should normally form a W to confirm a new bull market, unless other major indicators such as MACD and a price reversal at bullishly inclined moving averages also suggest a new bull trend.

3. On the *daily* chart, a market is overbought at a %K reading of 70 or higher and oversold at 30 or lower (as opposed to 80 and 20 respectively on the weekly chart).

    Look for the same general behavior of %K as on the weekly chart. However, in all but the most strongly trending markets, there are frequent swings between an overbought and an oversold condition, although extreme readings occur seldom.

    The four-price line doesn't have to form a W on the daily chart in order to enter a long position in a bull market after %K has turned up from an oversold condition.

4.   On both the weekly and the daily charts, an upturn in %K is a buy signal and a downturn is a sell signal—the same as turns in the other computer-based technical indicators. (Any seeming contradiction between using a %K turn in its overbought/oversold context and as a buy/sell signal is discussed in Chapter 18 on the entry checklist.)

Fluctuations in %K occur frequently, as they do for the single-price line. It therefore delivers many signals and often tips the balance in deciding whether to enter or to liquidate a trade.

5.   %K often provides a useful general indication of probable price action. When %K is rising, price is likely to work higher and vice versa when it is declining. An upward zigzag in %K may occur at a seemingly high level without impairing the prospect of a market going higher, and vice versa for a downward zigzag in a bear market.

When %K starts a downward zigzag in a bull market or an upward zigzag in a bear market before price turns, this *negative divergence* is the precursor of price changing direction. But the turn in price can sometimes take a surprisingly long time to occur because a %K overbought or oversold reading is simply an alert for a trend change. It can occur many times before the major, or even the minor, trend actually changes, depending on its strength.

To illustrate this point, Charts 7.1a and 7.1b show the weekly Canadian Dollar chart with stochastics, the four-price line, MACD, and the 25- and 40-week moving averages. Chart 7.1a shows seven times when %K turned down from a level above 80 and twelve times when it turned up from a level below 20. These turns are all marked on the bar chart (Chart 7.1b). The results, cross-referenced with the four price line and MACD, are shown in Figure 7.1.

We assumed that any %K downturn from a reading above 80 was a sell signal and any upturn from below 20 was a buy signal. The results were then tabulated for the %K signal (Column 4). Next we considered whether the four-price line, MACD and the moving averages gave confirming signals and noted the results (Columns 5 to 12). We assumed that a trade was entered if confirmed by at least two of the other four indicators (Column 13). (This is not a complete list of our indicators but it is a demonstration of coordinating %K with other indicators.) Finally, we examined the assumed trades to see whether they would have been profitable. In some cases, the assumptions about the success of a signal were subjective because they would have depended on how the trade was actually handled on the basis of the daily chart.

The results are summarised as follows:

	Profits	Losses	Total
%K Signal Alone	13 (68%)	6 (32%)	19 (100%)
%K Signal with Confirming Indicators	11 (100%)	0	11 (100%)

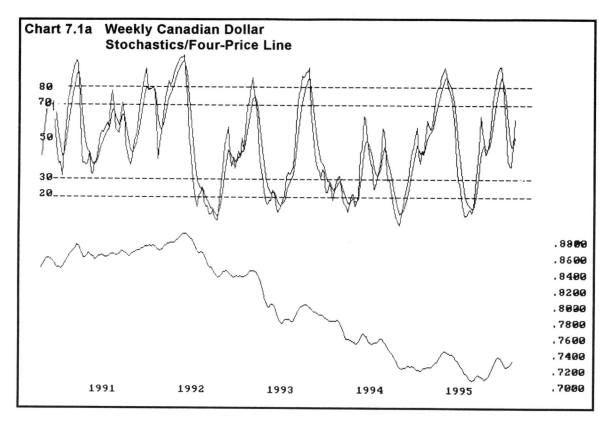

Chart 7.1a   Weekly Canadian Dollar
Stochastics/Four-Price Line

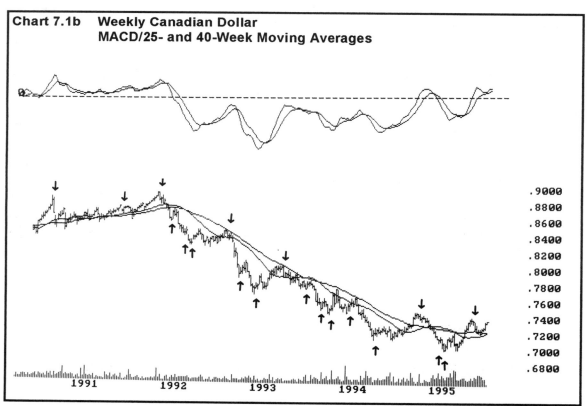

Chart 7.1b   Weekly Canadian Dollar
MACD/25- and 40-Week Moving Averages

Figure 7.1 Stochastic (%K) Signals on the Weekly Canadian Dollar Chart

		%K (Rounded)		Did Indicators Confirm %K Signal?									
High/Low	(1)	Week of Turn (2)	Was %K Signal Profitable? (3)	4-Price Line (4)	Week of Turn (5)	MACD (6)	Week of Turn (7)	25-Wk MA (8)	Week Confirmed (9)	40-Wk MA (10)	Week Confirmed (11)	Was Trade Taken? (12)	Was Trade Profitable? (13)
Overbought (>80) (Selling) Turn													
94	93	Aug 24/90	Yes	Yes	Aug 31	Yes	Aug 31	No		No		Yes	Yes
89	78	Jun 7/91	Yes	Yes	Jul 12	Yes	Jun 12	No		No		Yes	Yes
97	83	Nov 8/91	Yes	Yes	Nov 15	Yes	Nov 8	No		No		Yes	Yes
85	77	Aug 14/92	Yes	Yes	Aug 28	Yes	Sept 4	Yes	Aug 14	Yes	Aug 14	Yes	Yes
90	67	Apr 2/93	Yes	Yes	Apr 2	Unclear to Jun 4		Yes	Apr 2	Yes	Apr 2	Yes	Yes
90	87	Oct 7/94	Yes	Yes	Oct 14	Yes	Nov 4	No	Dec 23	Yes	Oct 7	Yes	Yes
90.88	90.72	May 19/95	Yes	Yes	May 26	Yes	Jun 6	No		Yes	Jun 2	Yes	Yes
Oversold (<20) (Buying) Turn													
15	21	Jan 3/92	No	No		No		No		No		No	
11	13	Feb 28/92	No	No		No		No		No		No	
8	19	Mar 27/92	Yes	Yes	Jun 5*	Yes	Apr 3	No		No		Yes	Unlikely
17	18	Oct 16/92	No	No		Barely	Oct 30	No		No		No	
12	14	Nov 27/92	Yes	Yes	Jan 29*	Yes	Dec 25	No		No		Yes	Yes
18	24	Jul 9/93	No	No		Barely	Jul 9	Barely	Jul 9	No		Unlikely	
12	17	Sep 10/93	No	No		No		No		No		No	
15	17	Oct 8/93	Yes	No		Yes	Oct 22	No		No		No	
7	30	Dec 31/93	Yes	Yes	Dec 24*	Yes	Dec 10	No		No		Yes	Yes
5	11	Apr 8/94	Yes	Yes	Aug 19*	Yes	May 13	No		No		Yes	Yes
10	11	Dec 30/94	No	No		No		No		No		No	
11	15	Jan 27/95	Yes	Yes	Mar 31*	Yes	Feb 3	No		No		Yes	Yes

* Date shown is when a W formation on the four-price line was first confirmed.

The results are difficult to accept as representative of what one might expect from a larger sample, since a 100 percent success rate just doesn't happen over time when trading futures. Even under the best of circumstances, the exercise of pulling the trigger may lead to missed trades or trades entered late that are subsequently stopped out. Despite these caveats, coordination of %K with our other computer-based technical indicators provides a highly reliable means of identifying major market turns. Note that the four buy signals were also judged profitable, despite the fact that the major trend for the Canadian Dollar during this period remained a bear market.

Figure 7.1 shows that:

1.   %K on the weekly chart does a superb job of identifying major trend changes when used in conjunction with other indicators. (In August 1990 and November 1991, this approach caught the crest of the market just as it was turning down.)

2.   %K also identifies the vulnerability of a market to a significant retracement when it is in overbought territory in a bull market and, as in the case of the Canadian Dollar, in oversold territory in a bear market.

The June 1994 Canadian Dollar chart shows several places where %K signaled a sell from overbought readings and a buy from oversold readings (Chart 7.2).

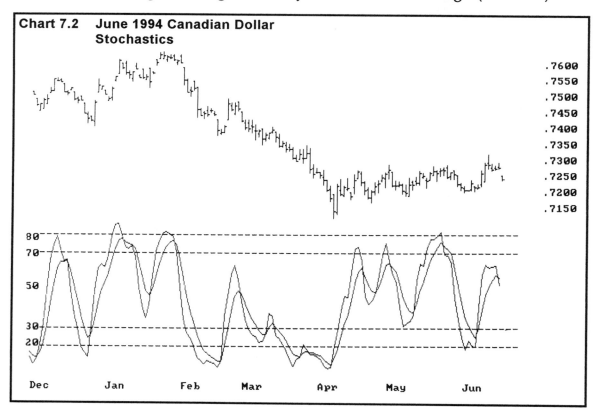

Chart 7.2   June 1994 Canadian Dollar Stochastics

A downturn of %K on December 9 was a good sell signal that was also confirmed on the weekly chart, unlike the January 5 sell signal that was not confirmed on the weekly chart. However, a sell signal at the %K downturn on January 25 was confirmed by %K on the weekly chart and by other indicators on both the daily and weekly charts. It resulted in an exceptionally profitable trade.

The apparent buy signals on February 9, February 16, March 7, March 19 and April 4 were all clearly contra-trend trades that were not confirmed by other indicators. In contrast, the downturns on February 24, March 10 and March 24 were confirmed by other indicators as new sales, although they occurred well below overbought levels. The signal on March 24, however, was canceled by the need to count a %K reading below 30 (at 19) as negating a new short position.

The June 1994 Canadian Dollar chart also shows a good example of negative divergence. %K peaked on January 4 at 86 and made a lower high at 81 on January 24, even though price was higher. Note, too, the enormous M that %K traced out.

At the bottom, %K did not demonstrate negative divergence. In fact, the %K low on April 1 was 8, one point lower than the March 18 low. However, it was apparent from this double bottom at a very low %K reading that price could be expected to turn up at any time.

We have now completed the discussion of our computer-generated technical indicators based on price: the four- and single-price lines, MACD, the 25- and 40-bar moving averages and stochastics. The next three chapters discuss how we use some of the non-computational tools of technical analysis.

Chapter 8

Trendlines and Channel Lines

Trendlines and channel lines stand the test of time. Most traders use them so their effectiveness becomes self-fulfilling. If you don't use them, you are at a disadvantage compared with those who do.

There are many variations on trendlines: speed lines, Gann lines, Andrews pitchfork, etc. Our computer-based technical indicators perform most of the job of determining which markets to be in and when. We therefore use only standard trend and channel lines, rather than any variants, when evaluating trades on the weekly and daily charts. Sometimes they can also give a valuable view of the very big picture when applied to the monthly continuation charts.

Drawing Trend and Channel Lines

A trendline may be short-term, connecting prices over just a few days or weeks. Particularly when a short-term trendline is steep, it is unlikely to remain intact for long. On the other hand, a very long-term trendline on a weekly or monthly chart may contain price fluctuations for many months or even years.

When a potential new trend starts, draw a trendline as soon as two highs or lows are clearly established and project it forward. (Trendlines always connect a succession of rising lows in an uptrend and a succession of lower highs in a downtrend.) The validity of the trendline is confirmed only when price returns to a point at or near the trendline and turns again, thereby establishing a third point of contact.

We like to draw a potential trendline as soon as possible because it is a visible reminder of a possible trend change. It may be necessary to redraw the trendline several times to express the direction and speed of the market as it develops. Frequently the initial trendline is too steep to allow for the inevitable price corrections. It normally takes at least six weeks before a correction occurs that allows for drawing a longer-lasting trendline.

Once you have a trendline that you expect to hold, draw a channel line by locating the point of furthest thrust away from the trendline and extending from it a line parallel with the assumed trendline.

The daily continuation chart for Gold from mid-1994 shows a succession of uptrends and downtrends, and the trend and channel lines drawn on it (Chart 8.1). The first trendline went from A to B and was projected forward. This trendline contained retracements until it was broken on a closing basis on October 7, when a new downtrend began. Once the line A - B was drawn, a channel line parallel with the trendline was projected forward from the high at C.

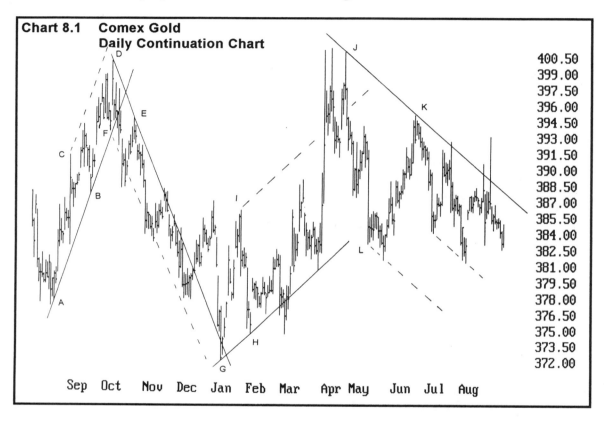

After the downside break in October, the market rallied to a retracement high that allowed for drawing the new potential downtrend line from D to E. With this downtrend line in place, a channel line was drawn from the low at F.

The lows at G and H led to a new uptrend line and a corresponding channel line from the high at I. Finally, a downtrend line from J to K and a channel line from L were drawn.

Using Trend and Channel Lines

Trend and channel lines have three functions for use in conjunction with our computer-generated indicators:

1.   Trend and channel lines illustrate a bull or bear trend simply and graphically. But when reasonable lines can't be drawn, that suggests the market is in a trading range.

Ideally, a trending market should move in a zigzag fashion from the trendline to the channel line and then correct back to the trendline. Retracements to the trendline potentially offer low-risk entries to buy in a bull trend and to sell in a bear trend. If price holds at the trendline, our computer-based indicators will generally confirm an entry. But if price fails to turn at the trendline or goes through it on a closing basis, that suggests that the trend is losing momentum or that it may be changing direction.

As a general rule, it pays to trade a market maintaining a steady trend, as defined by the major trendline, or a market gaining speed and requiring steeper trendlines.

2.   Trend and channel lines provide diagonal support and resistance respectively. Consequently, when a market retraces to the trendline, it is almost certainly oversold in a bull market or overbought in a bear market.

While the opportunity for lower risk entries at the trendline is a well-known principle, the idea of resistance at channel lines is less recognized. It can be all too easy to think that a bull market is taking flight or that a bear market can do nothing but plummet, only to find that it starts a vicious retracement from a level at or near the channel line.

3.   A trendline expresses the overall speed of the market. On a weekly chart, for example, you can see that a trade entered right on the trendline should continue to progress at so many points per week, on average, as long as the trendline remains intact. Price action within the channel shows the shorter term momentum of the market.

The daily continuation Gold chart shows how price worked up the channel from August to October but then failed to reach the channel line (Chart 8.1). After the failure, price collapsed through the trendline and established a new downtrend.
During the downtrend, each of the four lows had a successively weaker thrust, with the last one barely reaching the mid-point of the channel. This failure swing set up the market for a significant rally through the downtrend line and three months of sideways action before an attempted uptrend started. Although the price went through the channel line at the April high, it was unable to push higher and collapsed to the major uptrend line from the September 1993 low.

The monthly Gold chart is particularly interesting for the way a trendline drawn off the December 1987 high contained price until April 1993 (Chart 8.2).
From February 1990 to April 1993, price kept pushing against the downtrend line, with ever shallower trusts away from it, until it finally broke through powerfully. During the final stages of the downtrend, the trendline provided the only useful resistance against which to enter short sales and it performed a better job than the moving averages.

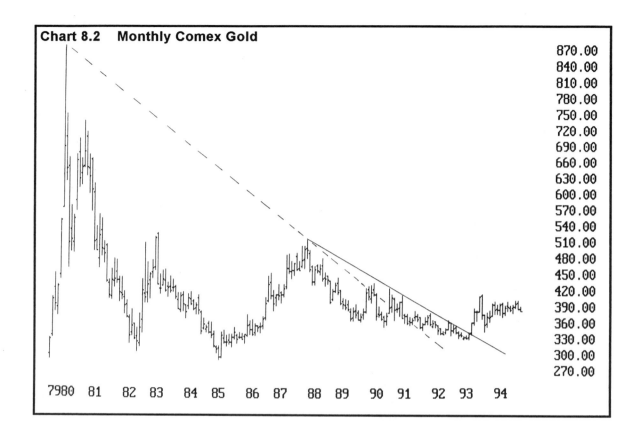

Chart 8.2   Monthly Comex Gold

Chapter 9

Breakpoints: Highs, Lows and Gaps

Support and resistance levels are provided by moving averages, and by trend and channel lines, as described in Chapters 6 and 8. This chapter discusses two kinds of *horizontal* support and resistance that we call *breakpoints*.

The first kind of breakpoint is the standard support or resistance confining the top or bottom of an identifiable range: the market has to break beyond that important level to maintain the existing trend after a consolidation or to establish a new trend. The second kind is the support or resistance created by gaps, when the market has broken away from a previous price level.

Historic Highs and Lows

Historic highs and lows are major support and resistance levels found on the monthly and weekly charts. Their importance is critical because, although unseen on daily charts, that is where they exert their immediate influence. The general rule is that, in extreme conditions, a market will be drawn toward an historic high or low, and can be expected to turn at or near that level. For example, in the last 20 years, Soybeans have found advances above 9.00 very difficult and short-lived, and declines below 4.75 impossible.

It is extremely useful to study monthly and weekly charts. Sometimes they can suggest developing opportunities well in advance of a market becoming a prime vehicle to trade. These charts always help to show how a potential trade fits into the big picture of price levels where the market is likely to run into resistance or find support. Therefore, it is very important to transfer major support and resistance lines and trendline points to the daily chart for any market currently traded, or contemplated, when price is within their possible range.

When price reaches such a support or resistance level, it will often retrace by an amount sufficient to justify liquidating a trade. By extension, these levels of support and resistance often provide prime entry points when the probabilities favor either a resumption of an established trend, or a major trend change.

Other traders look at long-term charts and know where the important support and resistance levels, and trend and channel line points are when trading. History tends to repeat itself. The probabilities, in general, are strongly against action being different the next time, unless the market has the immense power required to overcome major support or resistance. Even then, it seldom happens on the first attempt or even the second, but may do so on the third or fourth try.

The Five Star system does not explicitly use monthly charts as part of the process of entering and liquidating trades (as described in Chapters 17 to 19). You should know, though, that some traders monitor the monthly bar charts very closely, particularly as each month draws to a close, with a view to entering trades if these big-picture charts confirm the direction of a market. We therefore strongly recommend that you develop the practice of monitoring monthly charts. Always check them frequently as one month draws to a close and a new month starts. It is notable how often price action in many markets reverses near month end, often leading to price rule signals on the monthly charts.

In particular, watch for three price rule signals: price rule 6, trend continuation; price rule 5, Lindahl buy and sell signals, and price rule 8, double reversals. The latter two signals can indicate a major trend change, often followed by a powerful move in the new direction. This is because price rules 5 and 8 can take up to nine months to form on a monthly chart (for a Lindahl buy signal) and can therefore represent enormous base building or topping action. If you see such signals shaping up on the monthly chart, treat them as an alert to analyse the weekly and daily charts with a view to possibly entering or exiting that market when these charts provide the necessary signals.

Seven-Week Highs and Lows

One definition of a trending bull market is that it has made, or is currently making, a new high within the last seven weeks. The reverse, a new seven-week low, applies to a trending bear market. Therefore, any high or low that has withstood the test of seven or more weeks constitutes a level of support or resistance that could be significant.

A high or low that has withstood a test of many months is clearly more significant than one of only seven weeks' standing. However, we find that seven weeks provides a useful benchmark for distinguishing between fluctuations that are an exercise in backing and filling, and those that may have greater relevance.

We draw horizontal support and resistance lines on the weekly and daily charts at prominent highs and lows that have withstood our test of time. In addition, we draw support or resistance lines where there has been a market reversal powerful enough to suggest the possibility of a change of trend. Although the latter situation is more speculative, it is similar to the assumptions you must make about potential trendlines.

When considering the possibility that a new bull trend may be starting, seven weeks is often too short a period of base-building for price to move up through an important breakpoint, but it is not too short a period of time for a new bear trend to emerge when a break exceeds a previous seven-week low.

Gaps

Price gaps as levels of support or resistance are more complicated than prominent highs and lows but they are immensely valuable. They almost act like magic when combined with our other indicators. We like them when they are going our way and, paradoxically, when they are going against us!

Gaps indicate an imbalance of supply and demand. They show that no one wants to take the other side of a trade at previously acceptable price levels. The resulting price gap is a visible and reliable sign of the kind of market pressure that we want to follow. Adverse gaps are welcome because, even if it means having to book a loss, the call to action that they visibly give is positive. They are far better than a slowly shifting balance of supply and demand that can erode a position with grinding adverse action day after day.

We use gaps, together with our other indicators, in the following ways.

1. A gap occurs when there is a blank space between one bar and the next. *The Five Star system departs from conventional use by also identifying a gap when price draws away from the close of the previous bar.* (See Chapter 5, price rule 3, gaps, for illustrations of the two kinds of gaps.)

2. When price gaps, assume that there is support or resistance at the *closing* price from which the market has gapped, *provided that the breakaway holds on a closing basis.* Price often moves back into a gap to test whether the breakaway is genuine. And it often does so with an apparently strong close, suggesting that the gap is an aberration. But unless the previous close is taken out on a closing basis, this is one time when an apparently strong close is likely to be deceptive.

    Unless it clutters a chart unduly, draw a horizontal support or resistance line *at the closing price of the bar from which price has gapped*, when the gap has not been filled on a closing price basis for several days.

3. Gaps may set up a market for a significant move when:

    a)   several gaps in the same direction occur within a market consolidation; and

    b)   they occur at a breakpoint level (whether a prominent high or low, or a previous gap).

    When price gaps out of a consolidation area, many traders will have expected the breakpoint to hold and will be positioned accordingly. Sooner or later they will probably have to cover and may reverse their positions if the breakout follows through. A gap can therefore set in motion a bandwagon effect.

4. Gaps and limit moves in the direction of the trend *when a market is overbought or oversold* may be an expression of exhaustion rather than a continuation of the move.

The reversal from an exhaustion gap can be violent. The ultimate expression of an exhaustion gap occurs when price gaps one way and then gaps back in the opposite direction, leaving an island behind. Islands are one of the surest signs of a market's potential to reverse direction and they often occur at market tops or bottoms. They suggest that trading pressure in the previous direction has been completely exhausted.

Exit markets that deliver an island against a trade and look to enter a new trade in the direction of the gapping when other indicators confirm the entry.

5.   The 60-minute chart often shows a market setting up to open with a gap the next day. It can also show gaps more clearly than the daily chart. As well, deferred contracts, particularly in financial markets, frequently contain gaps not evident on the nearby daily chart, which can prove useful when considering the nearby.

When the closing bar for the day on the 60-minute chart, and other weekly and daily indicators suggest that the market could follow through the next day and start a worthwhile move, enter a trade on the close in anticipation of it gapping the next day. Alternatively, enter on the gap open, if the gap occurs.

When a close is very strong, especially a limit move, the benefits of trading into the close can be evident as soon as the next day's open. When the strength of the close is ambiguous, there may be a lower risk in waiting for the open the next day to see whether the follow-through occurs.

The April 1995 Live Hog Chart shows a large number of clear gaps and gaps that draw away from the previous close (Chart 9.1). We have drawn support and resistance lines from the most major of them. Note how efficiently several of them acted as breakpoints throughout the life of the contract.

Between late May and mid-June 1994, the market tried to rally through the breakpoints at 43.32 and 43.50. Failure to do so led to a short sale when price broke down on June 22 with the close at 42.55. Although there was little action between July and September, the breakaway gap down on September 28 led to a worthwhile follow-through.

The bottom occurred in late November with a textbook island and weekly upside reversal. The Five Star system would not normally take such a conspicuous contra-trend trade at that stage, given the lack of confirming indicators and the multiple layers of resistance. The ensuing rally topped out in January at 41.20, the identical price from which the market had gapped down seven months earlier!

Two months later, after a 3.5 cent decline, the market took another run at the top and this time managed to fill the gap at 41.20 on a closing basis. Despite the fact that the market had two consecutively higher closes above the 41.20 breakpoint—normally a confirming sign of a breakout, this was all that the extremely overbought market could do. The new high was a bull trap from which the market fell apart precipitously, with three breakaway gaps.

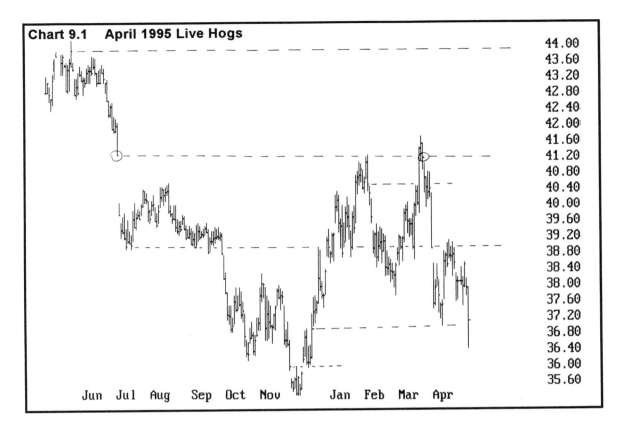

Chart 9.1   April 1995 Live Hogs

Gaps seldom move price far enough initially to satisfy the forces causing the gap. Therefore, trading with this signal can be very rewarding, particularly if you enter with the first gap out of a consolidation or from an island. Conversely, holding trades against the force of adverse gapping can be lethal, even when the closes are not particularly hostile.

Chapter 10

Breakouts: From Sideways to Rapidly Moving Markets

Futures markets often trade sideways for long periods—sometimes for many weeks or months—and then make big moves in surges. The Canadian Dollar and Wheat, discussed in earlier chapters, display both kinds of price action. The Canadian Dollar essentially went sideways from its August 1990 high at .8828 until its November 1991 high at .8902, a period of 14 months. Wheat was in a trading range from July 1990 to August 1991, from April to October 1993, and from March to August 1994.

One of the kinds of markets that we specifically seek to trade is rapidly moving markets. They often occur after a breakout from a sideways market, as in the examples of the Canadian Dollar and Wheat. One of the biggest errors of futures trading, though, is to assume the potential for a breakout and a subsequent rapid move before there is adequate evidence of this potential. The problem, therefore, is to identify the characteristics both of a breakout and of markets unlikely to break out or which offer inferior profit potential.

First, what to avoid: don't trade against clearly identifiable support or resistance levels unless you have an exceptionally strong case for doing so.

The characteristics of bull and bear market breakouts that we look for, in addition to our regular indicators, are discussed in the following two sections.

Bull Market Breakouts

1. A major bull market breakout generally requires a market to have made, or to be currently making, a new high within the last seven weeks.

The breakout in December 1994 Cotton occurred on October 25, with the close at 71.97 (Chart 10.1). This close exceeded the last high close at 71.64 on September 8, seven weeks earlier. It was also the highest close since July 25 at 73.80, over four months before.

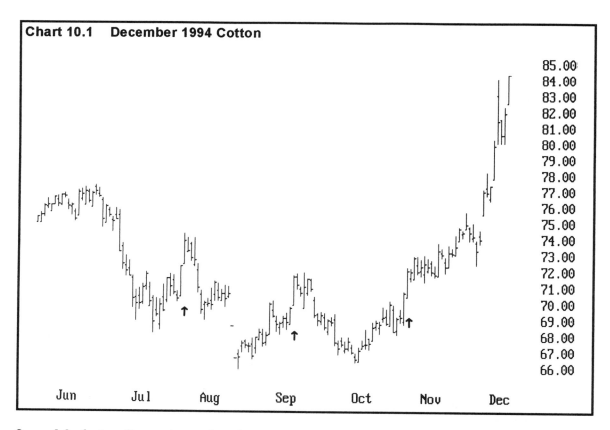

Chart 10.1   December 1994 Cotton

2.   Markets often retrace for three to six weeks. Therefore, the assumption of a potential breakout at six weeks or less may lead to an entry exactly at the point where the incipient breakout fails.

   Note the duration of the two incipient breakouts in Cotton in July and September that failed to follow through. Cotton reached a good level to sell, not to buy, when it seemed to be breaking out higher.

3.   A market is less likely to make a genuine upside breakout if it has made a new *low* within the previous seven weeks. This is not an invariable rule but it is an indication of erratic or bearish market action.

   The high closes in Cotton on July 25 and September 8 both occurred after a new low during the preceding seven weeks. On the other hand, the low on October 4 at 66.30 held above the August 16 low at 65.90.

4.   There is often a pattern of upward rounding on the daily chart; that is, an accumulation pattern in the form of higher highs and higher lows, or an ascending triangle that lines up the market for the breakout.

5.   A genuine breakout, as opposed to a bull trap, usually occurs in conjunction with powerful market action such as gaps, outside days and double reversals.

Also, there are often gaps and other powerful market action immediately before the breakout.

See the daily chart action immediately prior to Cotton's breakout: an upside reversal day, a consolidation day, an upside key reversal day, and a strong surge and close 137 points higher on the day of the breakout.

6.   The reliability of a bull market breakout generally increases in proportion to the length of time that the market has been going sideways within an identifiable trading range.

7.   A market seldom travels from the bottom of its range to the top en route to a breakout without a consolidation occurring on the way. A fast, big move within a trading range is not the same thing as a powerful breakout. And a market that does this will be quite overbought by the time that it reaches the top of the trading range. Therefore, the probabilities do not favor a breakout before a retracement, possibly a sharp one, occurs.

As well, the best breakouts generally occur after some hesitation at the breakout level caused by those who think that it won't break out, so that there is, in effect, a small base to support the breakout. There are often consolidation days following strong days when it is easy to start thinking that the buying power has disappeared.

8.   A breakout which takes the nearby contract to a new contract high has a very good probability of following through. The equilibrium of the market has been upset. Holders of short positions are potential buyers seeking to reduce losses. As well, the new contract high suggests that the supply/demand balance has shifted.

The July 1994 Coffee chart shows long-term basing action over a period of six months (Chart 10.2). Given that the weekly chart indicated that Coffee had been in a range below 87 cents for two years, there was a high probability that an upside breakout could take the market far, as and when it happened.

Coffee shows a slow rounding and acceleration with the higher January and March lows. It then gathered speed and led to the powerful breakout on April 28. This action took the contract to a new life-of-contract high, exceeding the previous high at 87.75 on September 10, 1993.

9.   Breakouts should normally occur in the nearby contract. When a deferred-month contract leads, it may be because of bear spreading. The probability is high that there may not be a worthwhile move up in any contract month.

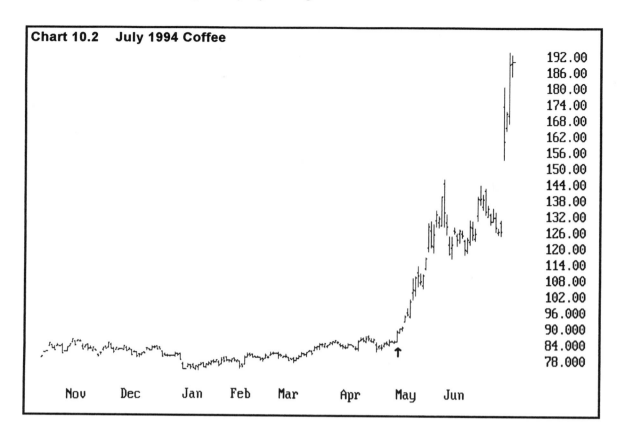

Bear Market Breakouts

Most of the characteristics of bull market breakouts hold for bear market breakouts. But there are some significant differences. In particular, we are more ready to sell high in anticipation of a market collapse than we are to buy low in anticipation of an upside breakout.

1. A major bear market breakout generally requires a market to have made, or to be currently making, a new low within the last seven weeks (the same principle as for a bull market breakout).

2. As with bull market breakouts, there are often market retracements of six weeks or less that do not lead to a downside breakout, or even to a trend reversal in a market that appears to be topping.

3. Unlike a bull market breakout, a bear market breakout often occurs after an intervening break out of the range *in the opposite direction* (making a trap).

June 1995 Live Hogs made an apparent breakdown low on February 10, exactly five weeks from the previous low (Chart 10.3). But the market rallied sharply instead of following through because the gap up on December 22 held as support. Subsequently, the March breakout was a bull trap that put in place the top of the market move. Once the marked failed at the upside breakout, it fell through support and crashed.

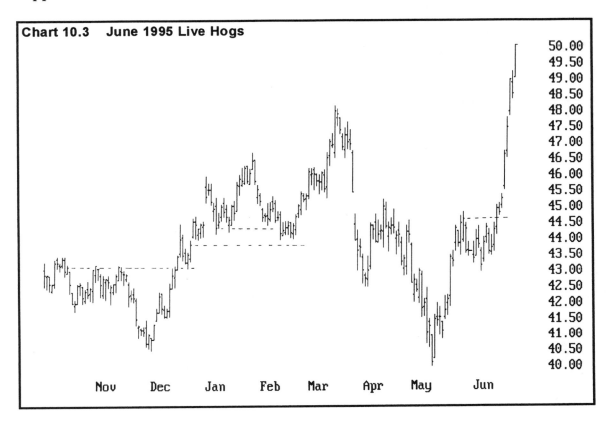

Chart 10.3 June 1995 Live Hogs

4. There is often a pattern of concave rounding on the daily chart; that is, a distribution pattern in the form of lower lows and lower highs, or a descending triangle prior to a downside break. Sometimes the daily chart can look like a river approaching a waterfall.

The sharp downside break in December 1994 Silver came out of a large descending triangle, which contained a small descending triangle with a steeper downtrend line (Chart 10.4).

5. A genuine breakout (as opposed to a bear trap) usually occurs in conjunction with gaps, downside key reversals or other powerful market action. There are often downside gaps within a consolidation prior to the breakdown.

6. Downside breaks occurring after a long period of sideways action have a particularly high probability of following through, the same principle as for bull market breakouts. (There may be, however, other reliable indicators for selling high, rather than waiting for a breakdown, such as a price rule 5, weekly Lindahl sell signal.)

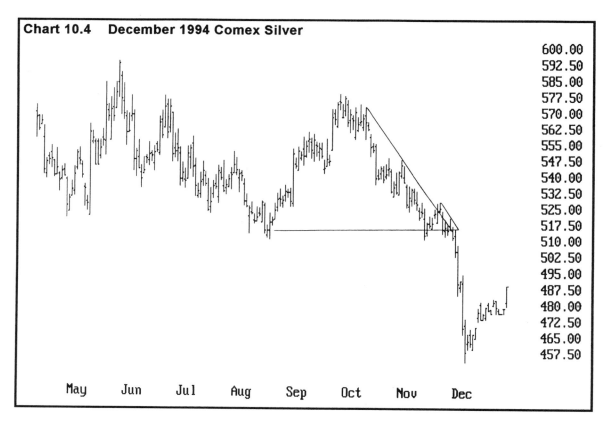

7.   Breakouts taking the nearby contract to a new life-of-contract low have a high probability of following through, the same principle as for bull market breakouts.

8.   As with bull market breakouts, the nearby contract generally shows the way if there is a conflict with the deferred.

There are more breakouts than there are opportunities for profit, let alone significant market moves.   In isolation, a breakout, even a seven-week or more breakout, does not in itself favor a trade, with the probabilities for profit below 50 per cent.   Worse, a failed breakout may take price right back to the other extremity of its trading range.   Even those breakouts that continue often retrace at some point to the breakout level or somewhat more.   On the other hand, all major moves start with a breakout at some point.   It is important, therefore, to know the conditions favorable to a successful breakout and to view them in the context of other indicators that enhance or diminish the probabilities of success.

One general rule applicable to all breakouts is worth repeating: *the longer a period of consolidation, the more likely it is that a breakout will lead to a substantial move.* Consequently, don't totally ignore markets that have been trading sideways for a long time.   Some day they are likely to surprise—and that is a key to a major move.

Chapter 11

60-Minute Charts:
Smart Money Clues

Chapter 5 described the price rules for entries and exits. This chapter applies these concepts to 60-minute charts in order to identify pre-emptive or anticipatory price rule signals.

If you don't have access to intraday bar charts, you can skip this chapter. For the Five Star system, this chapter provides some icing on the cake.

The 60-minute chart is similar to the four-price or single-price lines in that it removes much of the random clutter of the 5-minute bars. We use it as our primary basis for assessing market action during the day. We use the 5-minute chart for confirmation of action on the 60-minute chart but much of the time it merely reflects the random arrival of paper on the exchange floor, rather than the kind of persistence in buying or selling that we look for in the quest for bigger trades.

The 60-minute chart is particularly useful during the first and last hours of trading—when the smart money tends to trade. It can often show price action more clearly than the other charts, particularly gaps on the open or a market setting up for a gap.

Entry and Exit Signals

The computer-based technical indicators and other components of the Five Star system apply to 60-minute charts in the same manner as to weekly and daily charts. The 60-minute charts generally show the same gaps, trendlines, and support and resistance levels as on the daily charts. But they often also show additional price action, particularly for entries and exits. For example, a bar on a daily chart might show a close near the top of the range and suggest a high probability of the market continuing up the next day. Its 60-minute chart, on the other hand, might show that the high was made early in the day and that subsequent attempts to push higher were turned back, despite the close near the high for the day.

We look for the following price action on the 60-minute charts as *signals for potential entries or exits in markets with confirmed trends.* These price signals are, as usual, considered with our other indicators.

1.   Gaps with the Trend

The September 1995 Coffee chart (Chart 11.1a) shows a market that was known to be in a bear trend from its weekly continuation chart. Various indicators on the weekly and daily charts suggested by mid-May that the bear market rally from the December 1994 low might be about over.

On the 60-minute chart, price gapped down through major support around 165.00 at the open on May 23 (Chart 11.1b). This gap should not have been a surprise, however, because the final 60-minute bar on May 22 had dropped from 168.20 to 165.00 and closed at the bottom of the day's range. The 60-minute chart also gave other signals of this plunge, including opening gaps on May 18 and 22.

After a consolidation period with a downward bias, the gaps on June 23, when price opened at 149.10, and on June 30, with an open at 134.30, presented prime selling opportunities. Note that the gap on June 23 was preceded by action on the 60-minute chart on June 22 that suggested price was ready to continue lower.

Trading with the direction of a gap, especially when an island is left behind, can be very profitable. It is even better when a market can be entered with some assurance of its following through and possibly gapping on the next day's open on the basis of action on the 60-minute chart.

2.   Adverse Gaps: Gaps *against* the trend and, thus, potential liquidation signals.

The opening gap up on the 60-minute Coffee chart on June 21 at 152.50 left a two-day island behind, which suggested that a more significant retracement might be starting. However, %K on the 60-minute chart was above 80, and price was pressing against a downtrend line plus a breakpoint on the daily chart at 155.55 from June 15. In line with these indicators, the adverse gap on the open was negated on the close by a daily downside reversal.

3.   Islands

The 60-minute Coffee chart shows six islands to July 7. Three of them involve gaps with the trend (including the one on June 23 discussed in point 1) and three involve adverse gaps (including the one on June 21 described in point 2).

The most interesting island was created when price gapped up on the open on July 7. Compare the information contained in the daily bar with the bars of the 60-minute chart. The daily bar, although strong, might simply have been a test of the last gap down. In contrast, the 60-minute chart shows that price could not go much below the opening price during the first three hours, that it then turned strongly up and that price actually gapped up at the close, suggesting both great buying pressure on the close and the high probability of a follow-through the next day.

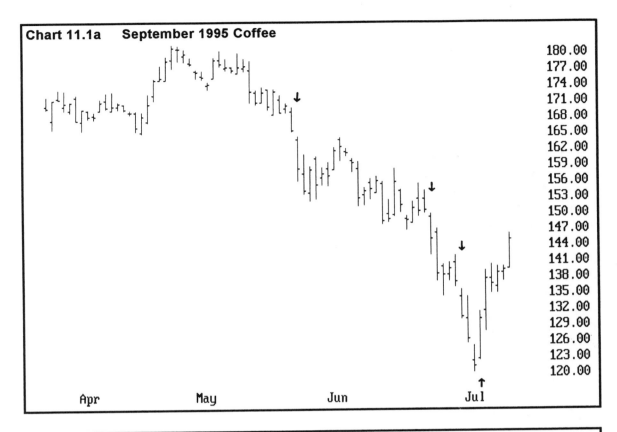

4.   Intraday Bar Formations, specifically:

   a)   price rule formations, especially ones completed with the final bar of the day;

   b)   key reversal bars; and

   c)   powerful bars that go through support or resistance.

On June 22 at 11:00 (Central Time), September Coffee completed a price rule 5 Lindahl sell signal and a rule 8 double reversal sell signal on the 60-minute chart at 152.30. From there the market slid to a close on the low at 149.80—250 points lower (worth $937.50 per contract) than when the signals were given. That was just the beginning, however, because the close at the low set the market up for a gap down the next day, June 23. A downside key reversal bar during the second hour of trading led to a further decline. On the next trading day, June 26, an outside down bar in the first hour of trading gave a price rule 2 reversal sell signal and set the stage for a further sharp decline that day.

The 400-point upside key reversal bar at the close of trading on June 27 correctly foretold the rally of an additional 400 points over the next couple of days. The decision whether to liquidate a trade on the June 27 close would depend on your personal trading style, given that the daily chart still looked all right. However, liquidation based on the 60-minute chart would have averted the stress of the retracement.

Market action on June 29 resulted in a succession of low closes on the 60-minute chart and a downside key reversal bar on the daily chart. Although the market held its low during the last two hours of trading, it was set up for the gap down of more than 200 points on the open the next day.

Price action on July 7 out of the low at 120.00 not only left behind an island but the 60-minute bars also delivered a price rule 5 Lindahl buy signal. The formation of valid price rule signals on the 60-minute charts is more common than you might think; there are others on Chart 11.1b that we have not identified.

The powerful closing bar on July 7 resulted in a close above the downtrend line from June 22. On July 8 the market tested the trendline until the closing hour, when it made a huge ten-point surge that reinforced the probability that the short- to medium-term trend had changed.

Other Uses

It is theoretically possible to transfer to the 60-minute charts the entire Five Star system of entries and exits by analysing them with the entry and exit checklists described in Chapters 18 and 19 (using the weekly column on the checklists for daily charts and the daily column for 60-minute charts). But this approach generally leads to many additional trades which make less money overall because of the cost of doing business.

There is one exception, however: Five Star signals on the 60-minute chart for the NYSE Composite Index tend to work reasonably well when it is trending strongly or when market action is fairly volatile. (Overnight trading in the S&P 500 Index tends to muddy the technical picture on its 60-minute chart.) Weekly and daily signals should be in force when entering a trade so as to avert the risk of a sudden resumption of the trend in its established direction. The 60-minute chart can be used for trading the Composite Index under strongly trending or volatile conditions because the Five Star system requires a market to move far enough after delivering an entry signal for there to be a profit in the middle when the exit signal occurs.

%K on the 60-minute chart often signals retracement turning points extremely well. It can therefore suggest entries early in a move or discourage entries when a market is vulnerable to a retracement. MACD on the 60-minute chart is highly reliable at showing the staying power of a trend.

But where there are conflicts between the computer-based technical indicators on the 60-minute chart and the daily chart—and there often are, the daily chart should be given precedence. For example, if the Composite Index on the daily chart appears to be setting up for a big decline but %K on the 60-minute chart is already under 30, it is critical that you not be deflected from the merits of the trade by this one factor. The market can plunge and %K can go to almost zero in such a case.

Finally, the 60-minute chart can be useful in helping to place stops, particularly for bigger or more volatile contracts such as stock index futures and the currencies (see Chapter 15, stop rules 3, 5 and 6). However, when trading smaller contracts or less volatile markets, the cost of doing business and the difficulty of making a good re-entry favors staying with stops based on the daily chart.

Chapter 12

Pre-emptive Entries and Exits: Stochastic/Gap Signals

This chapter describes a special class of entry and exit signals that we term stochastic/gap signals. They are based on the concept that a market which gaps, *particularly when starting from an overbought or an oversold condition, or when leaving an island behind,* is likely to continue in the direction of the gap. Stochastics (% K) indicate whether a market is in overbought or oversold territory and therefore has the potential for an abrupt turn in the opposite direction. Gapping provides the signal to pull the trigger.

Under certain conditions, stochastic/gap signals can provide pre-emptive or early signals for regular Five Star trades. However, they tend to have a higher proportion of unsuccessful trades than regular Five Star signals because they are pre-emptive. This shortcoming is balanced by placing very tight stops based on the signal so that losses or, in the case of exits, opportunity costs from taking signals that don't work can normally be kept small. If an initial position taken with a stochastic/gap signal starts to work, contracts can be added on completion of a Five Star entry signal.

Stochastic/gap signals occur at market opens and require immediate action. In order to use them, it is advisable to have access to pre-opening market calls, opening prices and, ideally, a quotation system with 60-minute, real-time charts.

Conditions Favoring Stochastic/Gap Signals

We look for stochastic/gap signals when conditions favor their being an early signal for a regular Five Star trade. This means looking for them when a turn may occur: at the possible end of a rally or a retracement, or at a potential change of a major trend. They can occur in all three kinds of market action that the Five Star system seeks to trade: established trends, rapidly moving markets and major trend changes. In the special case of vacuum crashes (described in Chapter 23), a stochastic/gap signal may be the only trigger signal for the trade.

There are several important technical signals which suggest that a turn may be shaping up. It is very important to understand that the probability of a successful stochastic/gap signal increases with the number of these signals present.

1. The four-price line on the *weekly* chart shows the potential for a double top or double bottom, or for an M or W formation.

2. %K on the weekly and/or daily chart is at an overbought or oversold level.

3. Price on the weekly and/or daily chart has retraced to a major support or resistance level, to an important trendline or channel line, and/or to or near the 25- or 40-bar moving average, and can therefore be expected to turn in the direction of the main trend.

Stochastic/Gap Signals

The Five Star system uses the weekly chart to determine the major trend of the market and the daily chart to determine when to enter a market in the direction of the trend and when to exit. Stochastic/gap signals occur on the daily chart. Valid signals occur only in the direction of the main trend, as qualified on the weekly chart.

1. When %K is at 30 or lower on the daily chart, buy when price opens above the previous day's close.

    When %K is at 70 or higher on the daily chart, sell when price opens below the previous day's close.

    This signal applies to both new entries and to the liquidation of existing trades. Action is to be taken on the open. Remember that a gap occurs when there is a blank space between one bar and the next one, or when price draws away from the close of the previous bar (described in Chapters 5 and 9).

2. When there is a *clear island* as a result of an opening gap, trade in the direction of the gap regardless of the %K reading. Here we use the conventional definition of an island—a clear space between bars both up and down, rather than just gaps versus closes. Ideally, the island consists of more than one day's trading action unless there is a strong trend, particularly a rapidly moving market.

3. When in doubt about the market's ability to stop and turn, wait for a second or third stochastic/gap signal before trading.

    Immediate market turns are more likely after a buying or selling climax exhausts the corresponding buying or selling pressure than after a long and persistent move. The law of series works for stochastic/gap trades: after each unsuccessful signal, the probabilities increasingly favor success with the next one.

4. For markets that trade around the clock, check the deferred contracts on the New York and Chicago opens if you are uncertain about whether a gap has occurred.

5. Allocate approximately 20 percent of exchange minimum margin for the stop, fine-tuned for a logical chart point which will probably be a very recent high or low.

    Tight stops are used for stochastic/gap trades because of their pre-emptive nature. If the stop is hit, it probably means that the market is not ready to move in the direction of the stochastic/gap trade.

6. Liquidate trades when:

    a) there is a signal to trade in the opposite direction; or

    b) there is significant adverse action during the current day; for example, an adverse reversal day or the gap that generated the entry signal is filled on a closing basis.

    If you make the wrong call, the subjectivity in deciding what constitutes adverse action is usually resolved very quickly by an adverse turn in %K or by activation of the stop.

Stochastic/Gap Trades in Practice

The July 1995 Soybean chart shows many instances of price gapping when %K was overbought or oversold (Chart 12.1). Those instances which coincided with the qualification of Soybeans on the weekly chart as a market to trade short in April, and subsequently long, resulted in four successful trades out of four.

The record of the four stochastic/gap trades in July 1995 Soybeans is shown below, excluding commissions and slippage, for only one contract on each of the four entries. (In real-time trading, the entry long on July 3 would have been in the August contract or beyond, but the July chart shows how the market acted.)

Entry Date	Long/Short	Entry Price	Exit Date	Exit Price	Profit/Loss
April 13	Short	597.50	April 20	579.50	$ 900
May 17	Long	576.50	May 23	600.00	1,175
June 13	Long	574.00	June 21	602.00	1,400
July 3	Long	581.50	July 18	635.25	2,687
					$6,152

The short sale on the open on April 13 was entered with %K at 80 and the appearance of a two-day island. It also coincided with a double top on the weekly continuation chart that developed into a second weekly downside reversal. At that point the 40-week moving average was still pointing down, although the 25-week moving average had turned up. If you had waited until the close of April 13 to enter, there was little left in the trade, as the biggest part of the move happened on the first day. Liquidation was prompted by a stochastic/gap signal to go long. The trade was not reversed because most weekly chart indicators suggested that the market was still in a bear trend.

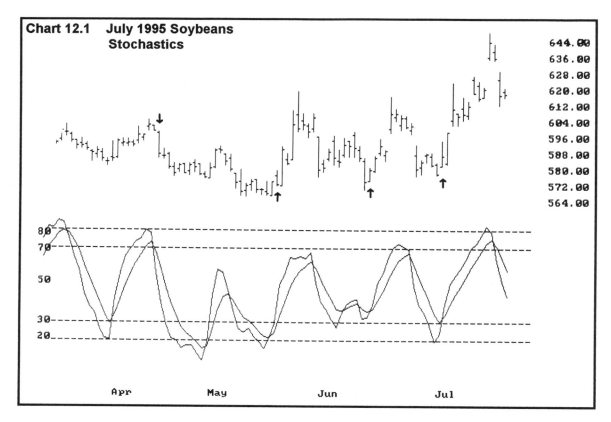

The buy signal on May 17 occurred the day after the delivery of a flat Lindahl buy signal (price rule 5), which could have been taken. The gap up on May 17 suggested that the trade might get moving, despite the flat Lindahl signal. Also, the moving averages on the weekly continuation chart were now rounding up. Liquidation was dictated by a big downside price reversal and a downturn by %K on the close of May 23.

The entry long on June 13 was on the basis of a gap up from the previous day's close. Although %K went to only 32 the previous day, it appeared to make a double bottom versus June 5, when it went to 27. Also, price did not close at the bottom. The trade was liquidated on a stochastic/gap sell signal on the open of June 21, although it was the second day with a lower gap opening. The first gap open might have been an aberration, given the strength of the market, but the second consecutive gap open, with %K at 72, had a high probability of signaling the end of the move.

The entry on July 3 occurred with a gap up after a double bottom and with %K at 20. Liquidation occurred on the close of July 18 rather than the open. Given the strength of the market, it was possible that the low open was no more than an aberration. However, after an apparent failure at resistance on the weekly chart and with a downturn in %K from 82 to 79, the low close strongly suggested that the move might be over. If the trade were held overnight, exit was mandatory on the gap down on the open the next day.

On over 20 occasions there were gap opens that might have been interpreted as stochastic/gap signals. But only the four discussed here met the conditions for valid stochastic/gap trades. While, on balance, the other signals would have been profitable, those which met the Five Star conditions caught the majority of the profits available from trading Soybeans during the period, and many riskier trades were avoided.

All the chapters to this point have discussed a wide variety of expressions of price movement. The next two chapters examine, from different perspectives, the actions of the market participants who drive price.

Chapter 13

Commitments of Traders:
The Changing Scene

Recent changes in market conditions make it more valuable than ever to analyse the Commitments of Traders (CoT) numbers. This is the published record of who holds what positions, and how many, in futures markets. During the early 1990s, a staggering weight of new money came into futures markets. Activity in financial markets, including interest rate futures, currencies and stock index futures, expanded exponentially, although some other markets such as Gold and the agriculturals mostly shrank.

The Non-Commercials, Commercials and Small Traders

Interpreting the CoT data involves subjective judgment and the circumstances in different markets can change over time. However, our experience has led to a number of observations about the three main categories of traders for which data is compiled: the non-commercials, the commercials and small traders.

The non-commercials, who are now mainly the investment funds, have such huge amounts of money to place that price swings are exaggerated in all the markets that they enter, and particularly in those with limited liquidity. Nonetheless, the principle of identifiable levels of support and resistance still works well. But the funds' buying or selling pressure may take a market to a second or third level of support or resistance before running out of steam. You must therefore be prepared to enter markets and to liquidate trades as soon as Five Star signals are given.

The funds have a bias toward the long side of markets. They are, perhaps more than ever, trend-followers in their intentions but they seem to be generally very poor trend-finders. Consequently, many fund-inspired rallies lead nowhere. The non-commercials often function as a prime contrary indicator when they have huge positions on one side of the market.

The commercials seem to have been trading more effectively than ever, taking the opposite side of the funds' positions at prices largely dictated by themselves. Trading with the commercials is not normally, however, a guide to finding markets to trade or to timing. Even when nothing is happening in Corn, for example, the commercials may have huge positions on both sides of the market, because they have to be in markets most of the time. You don't.

If the commercials believe they are right, they will sit out adverse price movements and add to their positions at their leisure. If they find they are wrong, they can reverse powerfully, thereby giving a further substantial push to the market's direction.

It used to be said that the small traders or non-reportables are always wrong. This is not true any more. They still have a perceptible bias toward the long side of markets and they tend to be wrong at extremes. But they are no longer a useful contrary indicator. One reason for the improvement in their performance may be the recent widespread use of home computers, good software and inexpensive end-of-day price quotations, which allows individuals to trade on a more equal basis with the professionals than in the past.

Using the CoT Data

The CoT data is published biweekly for each of the previous two weeks and is carried by various financial news services. In mid-1995, data amalgamating the numbers for futures and options positions began to be released one trading day after the data for futures alone. These numbers show the total extent of participation in each market. Whether traders will regard this data as more important than the futures data alone remains to be seen. Markets often react to the CoT numbers the trading day after their release when the data show very large or small positions held by one group of participants, particularly the non-commercials. The CoT data for futures alone may remain more popular as long as it is released earlier.

We use the form on the next page to record the data.* In order to track the changing picture of participation in each market, use a separate sheet for each one. We find that keeping the figures for only the most recent week is sufficient and that it takes 60 to 90 minutes every two weeks to record the figures and do the calculations for about 30 markets.

Here is a brief explanation of the columns on the form:

1. *Open Interest*: In very active markets, it is useful to check changes in open interest since the data was collected. The picture presented by the CoT data can sometimes be changed significantly by a subsequent major increase or decrease in open interest. However, record the open interest shown in the CoT.

2. % = Number for each long and short position ÷ open interest. Use the nearest round number. Some news services provide the percentage figures.

3. *Net* = % Long – % Short. Indicate "+" or "–".

4. ▲ = Previous net position – current net position. Indicate "+" or "–".

---

* The form is printed undersize for reproduction in this book. To use it, copy the form at about 120 percent to achieve the largest possible working area on an 8½" x 11" sheet.

COMMITMENTS OF TRADERS

Market																					
		NON-COMMERCIALS								**COMMERCIALS**								**SMALL TRADERS**			
		LONG		SHORT		Net			LONG		SHORT		Net			LONG		SHORT		Net	
Date	Open Interest	No.	%	No.	%		◄		No.	%	No.	%		◄		No.	%	No.	%		◄

When examining the CoT data, the following factors should be kept in mind:

1. Much of the CoT data is not particularly interesting in any individual week, but comparison of current data with historic data can provide useful insights. Look at the changes for recent reporting periods as well as for previous months and even years. Then you can see what constitutes a conspicuously high or low weighting for each group on either side of the market.

    Both absolute numbers and recent shifts in weighting can be significant. Further, huge shifts in CoT positions can occur extremely rapidly, particularly in the currencies.

2. The CoT numbers serve as a valuable contrary indicator when the funds are too heavily loaded on one side of the market. Some floor traders and others deliberately take positions against them after the release of CoT data showing these imbalances.

    As well, you can see when the funds' participation is getting near their maximum or minimum quantity in specific markets. When it is near the maximum, they are running out of fire-power to move the market further.

3. Someone must take the other side of every trade. The commercials, who are the largest participants in most markets, appear to act as the main offset for non-commercial and small trader buying and selling.

    The funds, like other speculators or investors, assume risk in the expectation of profit. Many of the commercials, notably hedgers, use futures to offload risk by locking in prices, which may mean locking in the profit that satisfies them; they don't have to be so greedy.

4. All futures markets are probably subject to insider manipulation some of the time, and some markets, such as Copper and Petroleum, most of the time. There is no restriction on traders acting on news available to them early but not yet generally known. Also, there are ploys such as those said to have been used for years by Russian Gold traders. They supposedly have routinely run up the price in the futures market in advance of big sales in the cash market.

The CoT numbers are an excellent contrary indicator, functioning somewhat similarly to overbought and oversold readings for stochastics. They seldom serve well as a timing indicator, except at absolute extremes, but they are invaluable for showing where the potential for major market moves may develop.

Chapter 14

Volume Indicators

The standard approach to volume is to assume that bull markets should have higher volume on up days and lower volume on down days. A bear market should have the reverse: higher volume on down days and lower volume on up days. There is also a saying that "volume precedes price". The idea is that smart money starts to build a position—or to liquidate one—before the market as a whole responds, and that this activity can be spotted in a divergence between volume and price.

We use two computer-based indicators to aid our reading of volume: on balance volume and accumulation/distribution. They are useful guides to the potential for an important change of trend and to the staying power of established trends in terms of what participants in the market are doing.

On balance volume (OBV) is a long-used indicator, shown as a single line for which no setting is required. To create the OBV indicator, a bar's volume is added to a cumulative sum when the closing price is higher than the close of the previous bar. When the closing price is lower, the bar's volume is subtracted from the sum.

OBV was originally created for the stock market (as were many other technical indicators). Some claim that this fact makes OBV unsuitable for futures markets but we have not found this to be the case. Volume is volume in both markets: for every trade there must be both a buyer and a seller.

Accumulation/distribution (A/D) is a more sophisticated version of OBV and is also shown as a single line. (The abbreviation A/D used here should not be confused with its use for the Advance/Decline line in the stock market.) To create an A/D line, a percentage of a bar's volume, based on (close –open)/(high – low), is added to a cumulative sum.

Why use two similar volume indicators? OBV is the more reliable indicator of buying and selling climaxes, especially when there is a second or third high or low in price that occurs with lower volume.

A/D is the more reliable trend indicator. It appears that smart money has a more significant impact on the difference between opening prices and closing prices than on day-to-day price changes. Smart money tends to use low opens as a buying opportunity in a bull market and high opens as a selling opportunity in a bear market.

Using On Balance Volume and Accumulation/Distribution

OBV and A/D give the best picture when used on the daily charts, although there can be distortions around contract changeover time. Also, there can be differences in the chart patterns for these indicators for different contract months when using software that utilises contract-specific volume. However, such differences can be useful to show different buying and selling pressures among contract months.

If the picture is unclear on the daily chart, it is useful to check the weekly chart. As well, when a market appears to be preparing to turn, it can be useful to monitor the 60-minute charts.

The same patterns of technical analysis can be applied to OBV and A/D as are used on price charts and on other technical indicators. Pay particular attention to rounding patterns and breakouts through previous prominent highs or lows. Because OBV and A/D are not based on scales or ranges, their level in relation to price is not meaningful.

When using the volume indicators, keep the following points in mind.

1.   If you believe there is an established trend in a market, OBV and A/D should generally track price. Minor divergences from one another and from price occur constantly.

2.   Following on point 1, when an established trend starts to weaken or shift, a corresponding change in the volume indicators is likely, though probably with less precision than our other computer-based technical indicators. A triple top or bottom in one or both indicators usually suggests that a shift in market forces is starting.

3.   When a market is setting up for a bigger move, whether from a trading range or not, the volume indicators may forecast the move well before price action. When there is a pronounced divergence between the volume indicators and price, the probabilities favor resolution of the conflict in the direction suggested by these indicators.

The weekly High Grade Copper chart provides a good example of how OBV and A/D perform (Chart 14.1). Once the bull market started in late 1993, both indicators began to track price closely, as they should if a good trend is under way. As the action shows, A/D tended to track price more closely than OBV, in line with its generally more reliable performance as a trend indicator.

OBV's action demonstrates how it tends to reflect buying and selling climaxes better. Note how it showed divergence at the late 1993 bottom of the bear market while A/D went lower. Similarly, OBV made a triple top with a marked downward zigzag in early 1995 while A/D made an almost flat double top.

Neither of the indicators forecast price moves well before price action, with the exception of OBV at the 1993 low. However, both of them gave a hint in April 1994 and May 1995 of the explosive price moves to come by the way they formed sharp V bottoms from which they moved up powerfully before price had moved very far.

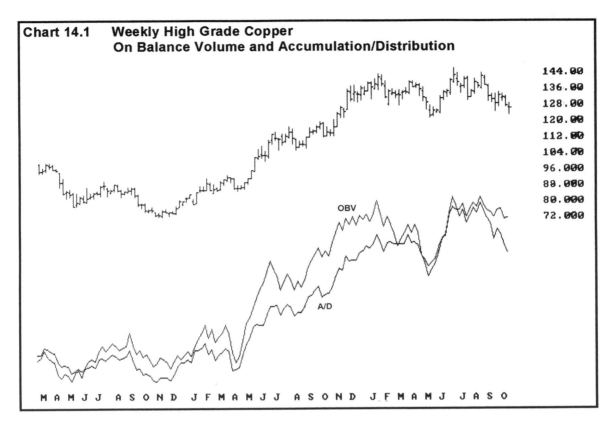

Chart 14.1   Weekly High Grade Copper
On Balance Volume and Accumulation/Distribution

144.00
136.00
128.00
120.00
112.00
104.00
96.000
88.000
80.000
72.000

OBV

A/D

M A M J J A S O N D J F M A M J J A S O N D J F M A M J J A S O

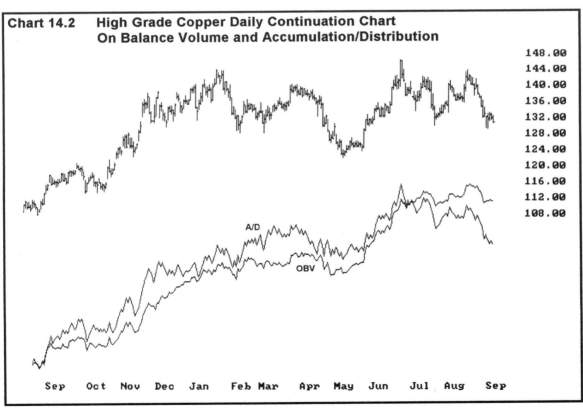

Chart 14.2   High Grade Copper Daily Continuation Chart
On Balance Volume and Accumulation/Distribution

148.00
144.00
140.00
136.00
132.00
128.00
124.00
120.00
116.00
112.00
108.00

A/D

OBV

Sep   Oct   Nov   Dec   Jan   Feb Mar   Apr   May   Jun   Jul   Aug   Sep

The indicators on the daily continuation chart for High Grade Copper (Chart 14.2, page 89) show a rather different picture from the weekly chart. The differences between their performance on the daily and weekly charts at the January 1995 high and May 1995 low are particularly striking. At the January 1995 high, OBV on the weekly chart performed the best in suggesting an important top and the severity of the decline from 142.90 to 121.50. This is a good example of an instance in which the weekly chart can clarify the daily.

On the other hand, OBV and A/D on the daily chart both started forecasting in April 1995 that the end of the decline in price was approaching. They therefore provided much more time to seek a good entry, based on our other indicators, than the sharp V bottom on the weekly chart.

OBV and A/D show patterns of buying and selling pressure in which you can place quite a lot of reliance when their patterns are clear. In a sense, they are almost psychological indicators that are useful to confirm or question your assumptions about market direction. An adverse move in price that is not accompanied by warnings from these indicators should help you stay in a trade that you might otherwise consider liquidating when other indicators are unclear. They can also serve to give advance warning to prepare for entry into a market with developing potential, or to prepare to liquidate a trade that is no longer drawing buying or selling pressure.

Chapter 15

Financial Indicators: Stops and Capital Management

Chapters 2 to 14 described the technical indicators that provide Five Star signals for entering and exiting trades. This chapter concerns the financial indicators that must be considered before deciding to enter a trade.

No matter how good a trade may look technically (and/or fundamentally), it is best to adopt the mindset that no futures trade is foolproof. This means that before entering a trade you must always know the answer to two questions: Where is the stop? and Can I afford the risk?

Deciding on and placing stops in the market is, at bottom, about managing your capital rationally. Stops allow you to put a handle on the approximate maximum budgeted loss that you can afford, including an allowance for commissions and a bad fill. They also serve as disaster insurance in order to protect the equity that allows you to stay in business. Although stops can sometimes seem to get hit at the worst possible price, they can also prevent massive losses.

Stop placement is discussed first and then capital management. You need to know how much money is involved if your initial protective stop is hit before you can decide how many contracts, if any, are appropriate for your account.

Principles

Our approach to stops is governed by three principles:

1. A stop should normally be in the market at all times for all trades. This approach imposes discipline on your trading and capital management.

2. Ordinary stops, as opposed to Stop Close Only (SCO) stops that are activated in the last five minutes of trading, are almost invariably better. While it is true that many violent swings don't hold, enough of them go further that the protection of an ordinary stop is preferable.

3. Even the best trending markets tend to fluctuate within ranges that are definable to a greater or lesser degree before they move from one level to the

next one. Stops should therefore not normally be placed within the apparent range of fluctuation where the probability of them being hit is substantial. However, we also believe in preserving profits. Our approach to stops placement thus tries to find a path between these two often conflicting considerations.

We use six rules to determine where to place stops in various markets.

Stop Rule 1: Logical Chart Point

Place a stop beyond a logical chart point on the daily chart, such as a price spike, a breakpoint or trendline, and/or a round number by adding a cushion of about $100 to $125.

Quite often a market will retrace to a level just short of a stop that has been placed slightly beyond a logical chart point. It will make a strong close against that support or resistance and then turn back with the trend on the open the next day. In such circumstances, it is necessary to choose between letting the stop do its job or possibly liquidating the trade on the next open. If the market opens with an adverse gap, it is usually preferable to liquidate immediately.

When the trend is strong but a stop is in danger of being hit on early follow-through action the next day, some traders prefer to lift the stop for the open. In that case, the suggested approach is to let the market open and see how it trades during the first hour. Then put the stop back where it was before or a couple of ticks beyond any further extremity reached during the first hour. If the market is trading at an adverse extremity beyond the stop point at the end of the first hour of trading, exit at the market.

Overriding stops is not a good practice but the practicality of real-time trading occasionally dictates doing so. There is a considerable risk that, in the long run, overriding stops leads to bigger losses or smaller profits because of the trades that get away on you.

Stop Rule 2: Dollar Amount

For an initial protective stop when the logical chart point is distant, use a dollar amount. The normal maximum amount should be:

1.   one-half to three-quarters of exchange minimum margin; or
2.   one-half to just inside a full limit move (see rule 6 for markets without limits).

Stop Rule 3: Inside Limit Stop

When the stop is beyond a limit move on the basis of a logical chart point, enter a stop just inside limit (based on the previous day's close) for the current day's trading in all but the most powerfully trending markets.

It may be possible to fine-tune this stop by using the 60-minute chart to determine a logical chart point within the range of a limit move. As with logical chart points on the daily chart, add a cushion if possible.

If a market retraces by more than about 90 percent of a limit move intra-day, it runs the risk of going to limit and locking there, and then continuing with a gap in the same direction the next day. It seldom pays to keep a trade through an adverse limit move, and then only if there is still a significant profit in the trade.

Stop Rule 4: After Limit/Failed Limit Move

When price has made a limit move or a failed limit move—that is, within about 90 to 95 percent of a limit move—in your favor, enter a tight stop: about one-third to one-half the value of a limit move from the most favorable point reached.

Failed limit moves have such a high probability of not following through that it often pays to liquidate near the close rather than wait for the highly likely setback to activate the stop. If the market looks like it will close, or has closed, lower than one-third to one-half the value of a limit move from the most favorable point reached, liquidate the trade by the close or on the next open.

Limit moves should lead to more limit moves. When a market stops making limit moves or fails to follow through to limit after trying, the probabilities are high that the extreme pressure on the market has been satisfied. One source of this pressure is the response of traders on the wrong side of the move who have been compelled to cover their positions. Once they have finished their forced liquidation, the market is vulnerable to a sharp reversal.

Sometimes a reversal from a point at or near a limit move in your favor occurs during the trading day. *In extended rapidly moving markets,* all or most of a limit move in your favor can occur early in the day. But once the pressure has lifted, a limit move can occur in the opposite direction. Therefore, when a trade in an extended rapidly moving market has reached or almost reached a limit move in your favor, enter a new stop during the day, based on the above parameters.

Markets that do not have limits or in which the front months trade without limits pose a problem when they are making limit-like moves, especially in very volatile conditions. See stop rule 6, markets without limits, for specific instructions.

Stop Rule 5: Price Target

When a market has reached a target price based on a previous significant support or resistance level, and/or when price and %K are very extended on the daily chart, enter a tight stop: about one-third to one-half the value of a limit move from the most favorable point reached (the same as for stop rule 4). This stop is intended to protect profits against the heightened possibility of a violent retracement.

It may be possible to fine-tune this stop by using the 60-minute chart to determine a tight stop more accurately, based on intra-day breakpoints.

Stop Rule 6: Markets Without Limits

Markets without limits or in which limits are larger than initial margin also tend to be markets in which substantial volatility or price fluctuations can occur without any technical harm being done to the main trend. Tight stops in such markets can result in frequent whiplash but loose stops can result in large capital losses. The following approach tries to find a reasonable path through this minefield.

a)   *In Established Trends:* Use stop rule 1, logical chart point, except for the circumstances described in (b) and (c).

b)   *Initial Protective Stop When the Logical Chart Point Is Distant:*

i)   one-half to three-quarters of exchange minimum margin; or

ii)   in the D-Mark and Swiss Franc about 100 points; in the Treasury Bond about one full point; in the S&P 500 from 200 to 500 points.

c)   *In Rapidly Moving Markets:* Use stop rule 1, logical chart point, normally.

If volatility increases or if the cushion of profit is not large, use the 60-minute chart to determine a tighter logical chart point than is evident on the daily chart. For those without access to 60-minute charts, consolidation areas which would provide logical chart points can be determined from your own or from your broker's five-minute charts.

Review stops and the current validity of every trade between the close and the next day's open. When in doubt about a trade, go through the exit checklist (Chapter 19). It is easy to overlook an exit signal when a market falters, and to rely on the stop to liquidate a trade. Particularly when there has been an adverse gap or a reversal day, it is essential to do a formal check on the continuing validity of a trade.

Another means of assessing the validity of a trade is to go through the *entry* checklist again (Chapter 18). Sometimes you will find that you shouldn't be in a trade and possibly should never have entered it. In that case, liquidate the trade at the market on the open: your trading capital must be preserved and can possibly be used elsewhere.

Managing Your Capital

As noted earlier, before entering a trade you must always answer two questions: Where is the stop? and Can I afford the risk? The previous section dealt with the first question; here we look at the second one.

Capital management concerns the amount of trading equity that should be set aside for each trade. Stops are not fail-safe and they sometimes get you out of a market at the absolute worst price before a market turns and resumes the move that you originally expected. As well, there can be market accidents causing huge moves that take price far beyond your stop before you can get out. Since you can make large amounts of money very rapidly in the best trades, there is nothing more important than avoiding ruinous losses that could destroy the ability to trade because your equity has been wiped out.

We therefore suggest several capital management guidelines:

1.   Budget to lose a certain percentage of the current value of the account if the stop is hit. This is the swing factor in determining how many contracts, if any, to trade.

We suggest using 5 percent of the current value of the account as the standard amount to budget for the potential loss on a single trade, with an absolute maximum of ten percent. Only budget for a loss greater than 5 percent when the entry signals are exceptionally strong and you are working with profits from previous profitable trades.

For example, you buy a Treasury Bond at 117.23, with the logical chart point stop at 116.13, risking 42 points worth $1,312. With an allowance for commissions and slippage, the trade on a full-size contract risks $1,450. This represents 4.8 percent of a $30,000 account. It is therefore appropriate to trade one contract.

This formula for determining the number of contracts to trade also requires a restriction on the number of markets to trade at any one time. We suggest a maximum of four markets, with a maximum risk of loss in the order of 20 percent of the current value of the account if every trade were stopped out. These maximums are in the upper end of the range compatible with keeping an account in business. Diversification frequently does not achieve the intended objective of limiting risk, but only spreads it.

2.   An alternative approach to capital management is:

Equity required for one contract   = Exchange margin x 3.

Equity available for additional
        contracts or other trades   = Total trading equity – Amount above.

If, for example, the margin on a Treasury Bond is $2,500:
$2,500 x 3   = $7,500.

If you have a $30,000 account:
$30,000 – $7,500 = $22,500 remaining equity.

No more than half the available equity according to this formula should be directed to the same market or the same general market area. Therefore, two Treasury Bond contracts is a reasonable maximum for a $30,000 account.

3.   Once you have met the financial test, you must ask yourself whether you can handle the psychological impact of the budgeted loss, if it has to be taken.

If you cannot meet both the financial and the psychological tests, reduce the number of contracts that you intend to trade or, if appropriate for a small account, trade a smaller contract such as a MidAmerica Treasury Bond or a CBOT Silver. Alternatively, you may have to pass the trade entirely if, for example, you cannot afford a six-cent move in Coffee.

4.   The most important factor in taking a trade should be the strength of the signal rather than the size of the financial commitment. The strongest signals almost always look hard to take while weak ones in more gently moving markets look easy. However, the probability of profit is often an inverse ratio to the apparent risk involved in taking a trade.

5.   Never take on more than you can afford to risk if the stop is hit *where the stop should be on the basis of a logical chart point.*

Entering a bigger commitment than you can afford and entering a tight stop is an invitation to lose money. All markets can fluctuate unexpectedly, and fluctuations between high and low breakpoints have to be regarded, in general, as normal market action.

On the other hand, entering a stop beyond where it should be because of preconceived ideas about a market is also an invitation to lose money. If the market exceeds its logical chart-point level, there is probably something about the market that will prevent its going in the expected direction—something that may not become known until later.

A very large number of traders do not make capital management an integral part of their trading program. If you don't, it is very likely that there will be large fluctuations in the value of the account, with drawdowns often exceeding gains. At the extreme, the probabilities are heavily weighted toward having the account go out of business. Consistency in making and banking profits in the long run wins out over banking large profits made erratically, as surely as Aesop's tortoise beat the hare past the post. With the Five Star system, you should be able to achieve big profits consistently, but you cannot expect to do so without a capital management program—one that fits your personality, your trading style, your financial situation and the certainty that there will be losses as well as profits.

Placing Stops in Practice

The March 1995 Cotton chart shows how all markets, including classic bull markets like this one, fluctuate within definable levels (Chart 15.1). It also shows the rationale for placing stops beyond logical chart points and the merits of moving stops closer when there are limit moves and failed limit moves.

Figure 15.1 summarises where the stops were placed from the initial entry long on the close of October 24 at 72.03; where long positions were liquidated by stop or market order, and where positions were reinstated on new entry signals. The Comments column indicates what price action necessitated a change in the placement of the stop.

The initial entry occurred with an upside key reversal. Given the power of this move, it was reasonable to expect the market to follow through. However, the entry signal would not be invalidated unless price exceeded by at least a small margin the entry day low. A retracement toward 70 cents could be an exercise in recoiling, prior to making a new upward thrust. Accordingly, the stop could be placed about 20 points below the low of the entry day and also just under the round

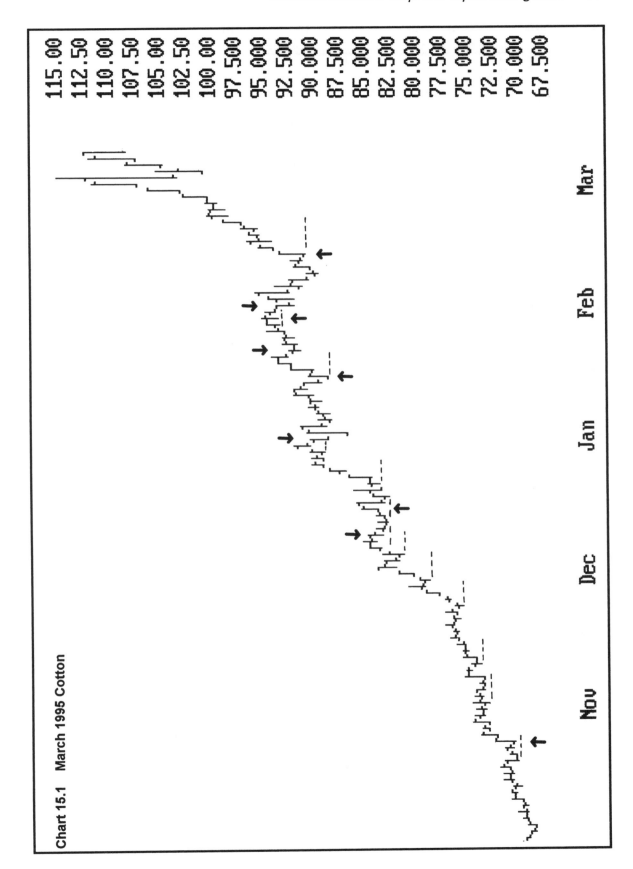

Chart 15.1   March 1995 Cotton

Figure 15.1   Placing Stops in March 1995 Cotton

Date	Close	%K	Chart-Point Stop	Actual Stop	Rule No.	Comments
10/24	72.03	74	69.95	70.10	3	
10/25	73.25	81	69.95	71.30	3	
10/26	73.15	84	69.95	71.20	3	
10/27	74.05	89	69.95	72.10	3	
11/01	73.63	85	72.45	72.45	1	Reversal
11/07	74.73	79	72.45	73.79	3	
11/09	73.85	72	72.45	72.45	1	
11/10	74.82	76	73.30	73.30	1	Island
11/15	75.95	83	73.30	73.99	3	
11/17	76.14	82	73.30	74.20	3	
11/23	76.78	80	74.95	74.95	1	Island
11/28	78.78	87	74.95	77.78	4	Limit
11/30	79.36	81	78.30	78.30	1	Reversal
12/01	81.36	87	78.30	80.35	4	Limit
12/06	82.34	87	80.75	80.75	1	Reversal
12/07	84.17	91	80.75	83.45	4	Failed Limit
12/09	Exit at 83.45					Stopped Out
12/15	84.88	78	82.25	82.95	3	Re-entry Day
12/16	83.17	68	82.25	82.95	1	
12/19	83.88	62	81.95	81.15	1	Reversal
12/22	86.18	67	81.95	85.18	4	Limit
12/23	88.18	78	82.95	87.18	4	Limit
12/27	89.60	84	82.95	87.65	4	
12/29	89.86	91	88.37	88.37	1	Reversal
12/30	90.35	89	Exit on low open			%K Downturn
01/17	89.95	65	87.95	87.95	1	Re-entry Day
01/18	91.82	76	87.95	90.95	4	Failed Limit
01/19	93.11	83	87.95	91.15	3	
01/23	Exit at 91.15					Stopped Out
01/30	94.35	87	92.70	92.70	1	Re-entry Day
02/01	Exit at 92.70					Stopped Out
02/13	92.99	40	90.30	91.04	3	Re-entry Day
2/14 to 2/27	Move the stop each day within a limit move					
02/28	Roll forward to the May contract					

number of 70 cents, say at 69.95. But this chart-point stop would be beyond the two-cent limit for Cotton for the next day's trading. The stop was therefore entered just inside limit down, at 70.10, in accordance with stop rule 3, inside limit stop. If the market retraced over the next few days, the stop would move down to, but no lower than, the logical chart point stop at 69.95.

As the market started working higher, inside limit stops (rule 3) were entered each day until November 1, which had a low at 72.65. This was an upside reversal day, although not a particularly strong one. Nevertheless, it permitted moving the stop to the logical chart point 20 points below the day's low (rule 1). Thereafter, stops were based on logical chart points and inside limit stops (stop rules 1 and 3).

After the limit up day on November 28, the stop was moved to 100 points below the close, in line with stop rule 4, after limit move. If the limit move were an expression of exhaustion and the market failed to follow through or retraced violently, the stop would protect most of the profit. After the market went limit up on December 7 but settled eight points below limit, the stop was placed at 83.45, about one-third of a limit move under the December 7 high.

On December 30 the high was up 174 points but price closed near the bottom of the day's range, an ominous sign suggesting exhaustion. This action shows why we monitor %K in even the most rapidly moving markets. On December 29 %K made a high at 91, equal with the level reached on December 7 immediately preceding a consolidation, and a level that sometimes precedes major market tops. On December 30 %K turned down, despite a new price high and a new high closing price. This is a good example of why we prefer %K to the RSI, which gave no such warning. (Stochastics are based on daily ranges, while the RSI is based only on closing prices.)

The downturn in %K provided the technical signal of a possible top and should have led to liquidation of long positions on the next open, particularly given a pre-opening call for a lower open. Alternatively, if liquidation was delayed, a stochastic/gap sell signal on the open would have required an immediate exit. Soon after the gap-down open the price plunged to limit down.

One conspicuously unsuccessful trade occurred as a result of an entry on January 30, at 94.21. There was nothing wrong with the entry signals as the market had broken out of a consolidation to a new high. The signals just didn't work. But it was much better to be stopped out at 92.70 with a moderate loss than to live through the major retracement to 89.20.

Using the 60-Minute Chart

The 60-minute chart can be used to fine-tune an inside limit stop (stop rule 3). But its best uses are to determine a logical chart point in very over-extended markets (stop rule 5) and in markets without limits (stop rule 6).

The December 1995 NYSE Composite Index chart shows the market potentially setting up to move to a new high after an upside key reversal with a strong close at 316.05 on October 17 (Chart 15.2a). Although overhead resistance at 317.15 remained from September, it was reasonable to assume that the market was ready to move higher following its 10-point decline and subsequent rally. The strong close on the 60-minute chart reinforced the expectation that the market could gap higher on the next open and run (Chart 15.2b). A trade on the next open could start with an initial protective stop under the 313.90 low for October 7, say at 313.45, which corresponded to a logical chart point on both the daily and the 60-minute charts.

The market broke through to a new high on October 18, retraced and consolidated, with a low on the 60-minute chart at 315.05, and closed strongly at 317.05 on October 19. The stop was therefore moved under the consolidation low, to 314.85.

The 60-minute chart shows clearly how the strong close on October 19 proved to be a bull trap. On the October 20 open, the market gapped down from the previous close and went lower during the day. The trade was stopped out during the last hour of trading. The market gapped down again on October 21, opening at 313.30 where the original stop at 313.45 would have been hit. Placing a stop in accordance with a logical chart point on the 60-minute chart reduced the loss by 140 points.

Stops based on the 60-minute chart are not recommended for use all the time. As a general rule, they lead to premature liquidation of too many good trades that would go on to make money if given room to move. However, they are a useful tool for the circumstances specified in stop rules 3, 5 and 6.

It is sometimes appropriate to use the 60-minute chart for a re-entry to a trade inadvertently taken out by a 60-minute chart stop. Otherwise, you can find yourself left behind waiting for re-entry signals based on the close of the daily bar.

Stop placement is probably the most difficult and frustrating area of futures trading. A trade stopped out that immediately turns and proceeds to move rapidly in the direction originally expected can be quite destabilizing. It is particularly frustrating if you have difficulty reinstating positions inadvertently stopped out. Nevertheless, a consistently applied program of stop placement will, over time, preserve most big profits and avert most big losses, thereby allowing for profitable trading in the long run.

The Five Star approach to stop placement, like all approaches, is certain to fail some of the time. However, we doubt that it is possible to devise a substantially better approach for general use. It is worth bearing in mind the saying that a trading system is only as good as its exit techniques, which often means, in practice, the care with which the trader actually applies those techniques.

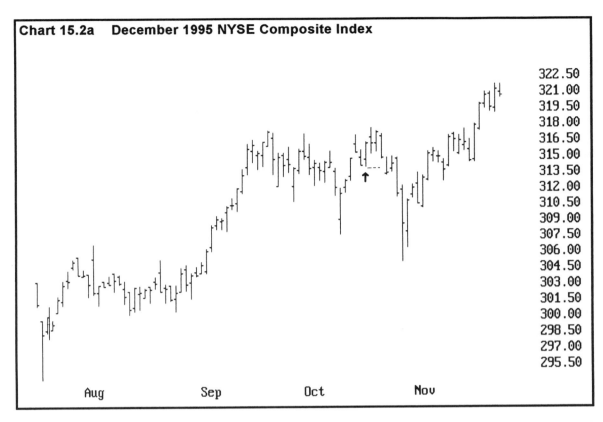

Chart 15.2a   December 1995 NYSE Composite Index

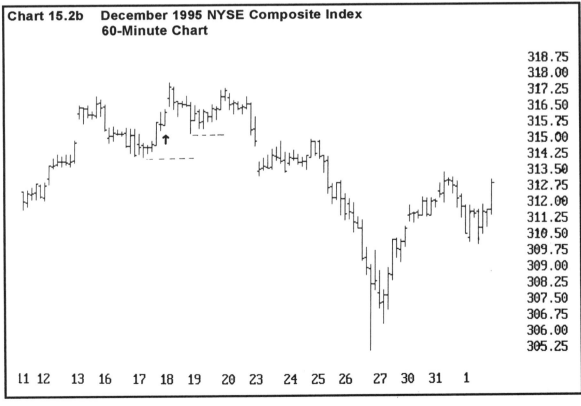

Chart 15.2b   December 1995 NYSE Composite Index
60-Minute Chart

Chapter 16

Finding the Best Trades

The Five Star system trades three kinds of market action, as described in Chapter 1: established trends, rapidly moving markets and major trend changes. In Chapters 2 to 15 we discussed the individual Five Star indicators. This chapter synthesizes the previous work by identifying the *prime entry indicators* for each type of market action.

These prime entry indicators should be most useful in three circumstances:

1. as a cross-reference when completing the daily market checklist (described in Chapter 17);

2. when you are uncertain about what a market is doing; for example, whether a market remains in an established trend or is undergoing a change of major trend; and

3. when you have been away from markets and need a quick and efficient way to review them by toggling through weekly charts looking for markets showing the prime entry indicators.

Established Trends

This is the most common type of market that we trade. However, it is easy to assume a bull or bear trend when the trend is actually sideways. It is also easy to buy high and sell low in a listless market that lacks the momentum to propel a trade beyond its entry price and on to a profit. We examine several indicators to try to identify established trends having enough momentum to be worth trading.

1. The four-price line on the *weekly* chart should have an overall pattern of higher highs and higher lows in a bull market and vice versa in a bear market. The highs and lows should have a readily identifiable incline. If they don't, it is probably a trading range market, which we seek to avoid.

   The four-price line on the *daily* chart only requires a turn in the direction of the intended trade for a valid signal, rather than a zigzag pattern. Some of the best trades occur after the four-price line has made a substantial contra-trend zigzag and then turned in the direction of the main trend, thus signaling the probable end of a retracement.

2. MACD's fast line on the weekly chart indicates the direction of the trend for the purpose of entering trades.   In an established and strong trend, there should be a zigzag in both MACD lines in the same direction as price.   The fast line should remain above the slow one in a bull market and below it in a bear market.   MACD often gives a warning of a major trend change long before the market actually turns, by rounding out and starting to zigzag in the opposite direction to price.

3. When %K is between overbought and oversold, stochastics generally trace out a zigzag pattern in the same direction as the trend.   When %K is either overbought or oversold, it may stay that way for some time, with divergence from price being the important factor to watch for.

4. The 25- and 40-week moving averages should have a clear upward or downward incline, with price trading above them in a bull market or below them in a bear market. Markets that make more than one close on the adverse side of the 40-week moving average are suspect and suggest the possibility of an impending trend change.

5. Trendlines show the major market direction.   Look for markets that require drawing steeper trendlines on the weekly chart, rather than shallower ones. A market requiring shallower trendlines shows that it is losing momentum and may be setting up for a trend change.   If you can't draw satisfactory trendlines on the weekly chart, there is no established trend.

6. A new high within seven weeks of the previous high should be made in an established bull market, and vice versa in a bear market.   If a market has made a major move, it may require longer than seven weeks to consolidate before moving on to the next level.

7. Entries having the highest probability of success occur when:

    a) on the *weekly* chart, a reversal or other price rule signal occurs at or near trending 25- or 40-week moving averages and/or an important trend-line;

    b) on the *daily* chart, a price rule signal occurs at or near trending 25- or 40-day moving averages and/or an important trendline; and

    c) ideally on both the weekly and daily charts, %K is oversold in a bull market or overbought in a bear market as a result of a price retracement. In a strongly trending market, %K may not retrace very much, if at all, on the weekly chart but it usually does several or even many times on the daily chart during the course of an established trending market.

Rapidly Moving Markets

It is usually obvious when a market is moving rapidly. It will be making strong moves day after day, often with gapping. Rapidly moving markets generally provide the best reward-to-risk ratio, provided that you correctly identify them and have the confidence to enter and exit trades exactly when it is timely to do so. Sometimes the optimum time and price entry occurs within the space of a few minutes, particularly near or on the close. If an entry on the close is missed, the trade can be entered on the open the next day, although often not at as good a price. But this should not deter you from trading; it is merely a symptom of a rapidly moving market and a good trade.

A market *with the potential to move rapidly* should have as many of the following features as possible:

1. rounding of highs or lows in the direction of the intended trade on both the weekly and daily charts;

2. a strong breakout from a long period of consolidation—the longer the better, and ideally occurring with a gap or a limit move;

3. gaps and, preferably, islands;

4. an absence of identifiable support or resistance to stop the market;

5. a breakout to a new contract high or low.

A market *already in rapid motion* can be entered with a high probability of an immediate profit (and low risk):

1. on completion of any price rule signal, but particularly a reversal—ideally, a *key* reversal—with the trend; or

2. on the first day of a break out of a consolidation, ideally occurring with a gap or a limit move.

Major Trend Changes

Major trend changes provide the opportunity to enter a market in the early stages of what may develop into a bigger move. The requirements for entering the early stages of a potential bull market are slightly different from those for a potential bear market.

An *emerging bull market* has the following prime characteristics *on the weekly chart*, which is the source for the direction of the major trend.

1. The four-price line has formed, or is currently forming, a W. When the second low is somewhat below the previous low, assume a valid W when either the four-price line or price (or both) exceeds its previous identifiable high.

Sometimes quite small wrinkles on the four-price line suffice to show the coiling action that provides the launch-pad for a move higher.

Turns made without a W, as defined, at bottoms on the weekly chart seldom have a good reward-to-risk ratio unless there are other extremely powerful confirming indicators, such as islands.

2.   MACD has been rounding upward for at least several weeks and preferably for several months.

3.   %K has been below 20, possibly many weeks ago, and has turned up above 20.

4.   The 25- and 40-week moving averages have clearly started to flatten or round out. They may not have actually turned up yet, although it is better if they have because they are an obvious directional indicator. Ideally, price has also crossed to the upside of upward inclining 25- and 40-week moving averages.

5.   A price rule 5 Lindahl buy signal and/or a price rule 8 double reversal is formed. (These price rules are particularly powerful because they involve coiling.)

An emerging bear market does not require an M on the weekly four-price line as a counterpart to a W for an emerging bull market. This is because market tops often form more quickly than the basing that generally occurs at major market bottoms. However, the best opportunities for short sales seldom occur without a valid sell signal from the four- and single-price lines, MACD, %K and a price rule.

We also distinguish between a top that takes time to unfold and one that involves a bubble bursting—what we call a vacuum crash. The special characteristics of a vacuum crash trade, like the collapse of the British Pound in September 1992, are discussed in Chapter 23. This kind of trade has the potential to make money more rapidly than any other trading opportunity. However, such opportunities occur, at most, only a few times a year. When they do, they require the fullest attention to our prime vacuum crash indicators and a readiness both to enter and exit trades exactly when it is timely to do so.

The next section summarizes the most critical Five Star indicators. We have put it on a separate page so that you may, if you wish, easily copy and post it as a useful reminder during your searches for the best trades. If trades were taken only when one or more of these signals occurred, subject to Form 2, Five Star Entry Checklist (Chapter 18), some big trades would be missed. But such an approach should catch a majority of the big moves and, at least as important, reduce the number of losing trades significantly.

Following this section, Chapters 17, 18 and 19 describe how to use all the indicators to identify and to liquidate trades by completing the Five Star checklists.

Top Five Star Indicators

There is almost always a substantial trade, subject to confirmation on Form 2, entry checklist, under any of the following five conditions:

1. On the *weekly* chart, %K is, or has recently been, above 80 or below 20, and has turned in the direction of the intended trade; *and*

   a) the four-price line forms a clear M or W, *or*

   b) a price rule 5, Lindahl or rule 8, double reversal signal occurs.

2. On the *weekly* chart, a price rule signal (including a single bar that qualifies as a rule 6, trend continuation signal) occurs at or near the 25- or 40-week moving average, and/or a prominent trendline, which is pointing in the direction of the intended trade.

   The moving averages often turn at different times. It is sufficient for one of them to indicate the direction of the assumed trend, although it is preferable that they both do so.

   It is usually obvious whether a non-confirming moving average is rounding and preparing to turn in the same direction as the one already signaling the direction of the intended trade. The steeper the incline of the moving averages and/or the trendline, the better.

3. On the *daily* chart, a price rule signal occurs in the same manner as on the weekly chart (point 2). The market must also be qualified to trade on the basis of the weekly chart.

   When this signal is given, a market may not look promising because it will usually have just undergone a substantial retracement. But the price rule signal suggests a turn and markets often turn strongly after a major retracement because they have wrung out many participants. Therefore, the potential for gain is great while the risk of loss is limited.

4. A breakout occurs from a consolidation—the longer, the better—combined with:

   a) rounding of price bars and/or indicators such as the four-price line and MACD; *and*

   b) powerful daily price action, especially gapping on the breakout.

5. In a *rapidly moving market*, a reversal day, especially a key reversal, occurs in the direction of the trend.

When any of these signals occur, seize the moment and do an analysis of the weekly and daily charts, using Form 2. Any one of these signals constitutes the nearest thing to an "always trade" alert. When more than one of them occur at the same time, the probabilities of a successful trade are even more favorable.

Chapter 17

Daily Market Checklist

Futures traders often say, "Why didn't I buy (or sell) that market? I had a good signal but I didn't act on it." Often the question results from not having actually seen the signal when it was timely. A timely entry can occur within a very short window of opportunity, sometimes no later than the market open following the day of the signal. You can't trade what you don't see and if you often see signals only after the event, you're likely to gnash a lot of teeth.

Markets having the best profit potential are often ones that come to life suddenly, after a period of trading sideways. Superb entry points can also occur when a market abruptly finishes a retracement to a level where a turn can be expected, such as a moving average or a trendline. The best way of spotting opportunities when they occur is to have a means of quickly checking all markets daily to identify the ones that may be delivering prime entry or exit signals.

Form 1, Five Star Daily Market Checklist

Use Form 1, Five Star Daily Market Checklist to obtain a rapid summary of all markets every day, by reviewing a few key indicators. Then, for any market which this quick check identifies as possibly shaping up for action, do a detailed analysis using the Five Star entry or exit checklists, described in Chapters 18 and 19. In practice, you may find it possible to skip certain markets on Form 1 when it is clear that there is no trade.

Each column on Form 1 is described below.*

1. *Mkts. (Markets):* This column is blank to allow you to list the markets that you follow in your preferred order.

2. *Daily %K (Daily Chart, %K):* Enter the nearest round number. This is the first alert for a market having the potential to make a sharp turn, although it may be long delayed in a rapidly moving market.

---

* You may find it useful to copy Forms 1, 2 and 3 at about 115 percent.

Form 1   Five Star DAILY MARKET Checklist   Date:_____

Mkts.	Daily % K	Daily Rev.	Turn MA/TL	Gaps/ Islands	Wkly %K	Wkly Rev.	Turn MA/TL	60-Min.	Action

3. *Daily Rev. (Daily Price Reversal):* When a reversal occurs, make a tick with a plus sign for an upside reversal and with a minus sign for a downside reversal. A single reversal day may not be meaningful but check how it fits into the larger picture. In a rapidly moving market, a single reversal day with the trend usually signals a timely entry with a manageable stop. A single reversal day at or near clearly trending moving averages, or a trendline may signal the end of a retracement and the start of a new move in the direction of the trend.

4. *Turn MA/TL (Price Turn at Trending 25- and/or 40-**Day** Moving Averages, and/or an Important Trendline):* A price turn may occur with only a single reversal day with the trend. The most profitable turns occur with an emerging or actual price rule signal at a moving average or an important trendline. There are relatively few such turns. When they occur, they are often the nearest thing to a "must trade" alert.

5. *Gaps/Islands (Daily and Weekly Charts):* Count an unfilled gap from the previous close and islands. All gaps are extremely important in suggesting the possibility of the market continuing in the direction of the gapping. Make a tick with a plus sign for a gap up and with a minus sign for a gap down.

6. *Wkly %K (Weekly Chart, %K):* Enter the nearest round number.

7. Wkly Rev. (Weekly Price Reversal): Unless it is the last trading day of the week, make an assumption about the potential for a weekly reversal as if it were the last day. A weekly reversal is extremely important, particularly when there is more than one or when it occurs at or near trending moving averages and/or an important trendline.

8. *Turn MA/TL (Price Turn at Trending 25- and/or 40-**Week** Moving Averages, and/or an Important Trendline):* This is potentially one of the most powerful of all signals for a major market move. Follow up on the entry checklist.

9. *60-Min. (60-Minute Chart):* If other indicators look interesting, does the 60-minute chart suggest the possibility of follow-through? Or is the chart actually suggesting exhaustion rather than continuation?

10. *Action:* Indicate which markets appear to merit further analysis for a potential entry or exit, using the entry checklist (Form 2, Chapter 18) or the exit checklist (Form 3, Chapter 19).

The primary orientation of the daily market checklist may seem to be toward entries. But it is at least as important to use Form 1 as an alert for existing trades that may need to be liquidated.

Chapter 18

Entry Checklist:
Bringing Together the Signals

You have gone through the daily market checklist and identified a market that appears to have trading potential. This chapter shows how to analyse such a market, using Form 2, Five Star Entry Checklist. Using the entry checklist makes the material manageable and the process of entering markets objective.

There are several columns on the checklist to allow for subsequent analyses if the initial check does not signal a trade, and to monitor a trade once it is entered. For example, you may want to add contracts, especially on completion of a reversal day in a rapidly moving market. The daily chart portion of the form has more columns than the weekly portion because a market can qualify to trade on the weekly chart some time before it does so on the daily chart.

You will sometimes find that continuing to hold a trade can no longer be justified on the basis of the entry checklist. This occurs mainly in cases where you expected a market to follow through but it has lapsed into a trading range instead.

The weekly continuation chart and the weekly chart for the contract you want to trade can show substantial differences in price and therefore in indicator readings. In the agriculturals, there can be large differences between the price of the nearest futures contract and the next contract, especially when they represent different crop years. In such cases, it is usually preferable to rely on the weekly chart for the contract to be traded, particularly around contract changeover time. If a contract-specific weekly chart is not available, look for weekly reversals and other price rule signals by examining the daily chart carefully.

Form 2, Confirming Indicators

Each of the confirming indicators on the entry checklist is described below. First, examine these indicators on the *weekly* chart. It takes a net total of five confirming weekly indicators (confirming indicators minus negating ones) to *qualify* a market for a potential Five Star trade. If the potential trade qualifies on the weekly chart, examine the indicators on the daily chart to determine if the trade should be entered.

Form 2   Five Star ENTRY Checklist

Contract:_____ Buy:_____ Sell:_____ Date Started: _____

	Weekly Chart					Daily Chart				
Confirming Indicators										
Date										
1. Four-Price Line										
2. Single-Price Line										
3. MACD										
4. % K Turn										
5. 25- Bar MA Direction										
6. 40-Bar MA Direction										
7. Price Rule Signal										
8. Reversal at MA/Trendline										
9. Key Reversal										
10. Double Reversal										
11. Gap										
12. Island [1]										
Total										
Negating Indicators										
1. Adverse %K Level [2]										
2. Adverse Gap(s) [3]										
3. Adverse Breakpoint										
4. Adverse Channel Line										
5. Double Top/Bottom										
6. Adverse Trendline										
Total										
NET CONFIRMING INDICATORS (Confirming – Negating: 5 needed on both weekly & daily for entry)[4]										
Other Indicators										
1. 60-Minute Chart										
2. Commitments of Traders										
3. On Balance Volume										
4. Accumulation/Distribution										
5. Backwardation										
6. Stop/Capital Management										

[1]   If an island occurs only on the *daily* chart, also count it on the *weekly* chart.

[2]   If %K is >80 or <20 on the weekly chart and/or >70 or <30 on the daily chart, count as a negating indicator.

[3]   Enter one check for each adverse gap that remains unfilled on a closing basis during the most recent consolidation.

[4]   For a potential *major trend change*, confirming indicators 1, 2, 3, 4 and 7 on the weekly and daily charts should confirm.

Use a tick when an indicator confirms action, an X when it negates it and leave the space blank when it is not applicable.

When assuming a major market turn, as opposed to the continuation of an established trend or a rapidly moving market, the first four technical indicators on the checklist—the four- and single-price lines, MACD and %K—plus a price rule signal should normally all confirm entry on the weekly chart.

For all kinds of market action, the confirming indicators should normally include a price rule signal on both the weekly and the daily charts. This stipulation may be overridden only when other indicators are very favorable. You might, for example, pre-emptively assume that a price rule signal will be delivered when price appears to be turning at major support or resistance within a strong, established trend.

Some of the indicators may result in double (or more) counting, as when there is a price rule signal plus a double reversal, a key reversal or a gap. This approach intentionally gives additional weighting to these indicators.

The description of the confirming indicators on Form 2 follows.

1. *Four-Price Line:* On the *weekly* chart when *buying*, the four-price line has formed, or is currently forming, a W. When the second low is somewhat below the previous low, assume a valid W when the four-price line or price (or both) exceeds its previous identifiable high.

    On the *daily* chart when *buying*, the four-price line turns up.

    On the weekly and daily charts when *selling*, the four-price line turns down. A corresponding M is not required, provided that other indicators, especially a previously overbought %K, confirm the trade.

2. *Single-Price Line:* Turns in the direction of the intended trade. When there is ambiguity about interpreting the direction of the *four-price* line, the single-price line sometimes makes a zigzag that helps to clarify the analysis of market potential.

3. *MACD:* Fast line turns in the direction of the intended trade.

4. *%K Turn:* Turns in the direction of the intended trade. Note whether the market is significantly overbought or oversold (weekly chart: >80, <20; daily chart: >70, <30). The general principle is to buy an oversold market and to sell an overbought one.

    For trades at potential major market turns (rather than those in an established trend or in a rapidly moving market), see Chapter 7 for an explanation of the most favorable circumstances for turns.

5. *25-Bar Moving Average (MA) Direction:* Points in the direction of the intended trade.

6. *40-Bar Moving Average (MA) Direction:* Points in the direction of the intended trade.

7. *Price Rule Signal*: See Chapter 5 for the eight rules. A single weekly price reversal counts as a confirming price rule 6, trend continuation signal on the weekly checklist when the trend is confirmed by either the 25- or 40-week moving average.

8. *Reversal at Moving Average/Trendline: Any of the price rule signals* shows a price reversal at or near the 25- or 40-bar moving average and/or an important trendline, and in their direction. When both moving averages are pointing in the direction of the intended trade, the probability of the trend continuing is extremely high.

9. *Key Reversal (Price Rule 2)*: Points in the direction of the intended trade. Price closes in the top or bottom 25 percent, as appropriate, of the bar's range.

10. *Double Reversal (Price Rule 8)*: Points in the direction of the intended trade. Price closes in the top or bottom 25 percent, as appropriate, of both bars' ranges. Ideally, when buying, the second low and close should be higher. When selling, the second high and close should be lower.

11. *Gap (Price Rule 3)*: Occurs when there is a blank space between one bar and the next one or when price draws away from the close of the previous bar and fails to fill the gap on a closing basis.

     When there is more than one gap, count only one (unless there is also an island). Each additional gap takes price nearer to the end of its move. The strength of other indicators generally shows whether there is still a favorable reward-to-risk ratio.

12. *Island (Price Rule 4)*: Occurs when there is a blank space on the chart as a result of price first gapping up and then down, or vice versa. It also occurs when there is gapping away from closes first in one direction and then in the other, even if the ranges of two or more bars overlap. The more time taken to form an island and the more symmetrical it is, the more likely that there is an important turning point.

     Because an island occurs with a gap, count both points 11 and 12. If an island occurs only on the daily chart, also count it on the weekly chart checklist.

Form 2, Negating Indicators

The presence of negating indicators is an immediate reason for caution. Even one negating indicator requires taking extra care in evaluating a potential trade. For example, the probabilities in favor of a trade's success fall significantly when buying immediately below a clear breakpoint or selling immediately above one. But the existence of an adverse breakpoint is not sufficient to preclude a trade if, for example, there is a key reversal in the direction of the assumed trend.

1. *%K Level*: On the *weekly* chart, %K is or has recently been at or above 80, if long, or at or below 20, if short.

   On the *daily* chart, %K is or has recently been at or above 70, if long, or at or below 30, if short.

   The negative implications of an overbought or oversold %K level have to be tempered with the recognition that the most powerful moves result in extreme stochastics readings very early in the move. However, there will generally be many confirming indicators to override a negative %K reading if the trade has potential.

2. *Adverse Gap(s) (Price Rule 3)*: Enter one tick for each adverse gap that remains unfilled on a closing basis during the most recent consolidation or formation. Gaps standing in the way of an intended trade can represent a breakpoint at which the market is likely to be turned back. When there are gaps both above and below the market, there is considerable indecision and market action may be very erratic until price breaks beyond the consolidation range.

3. *Adverse Breakpoint*: Occurs *when price is near* an important support or resistance level, including an adverse gap, that stands in the way of the intended trade.

   When there is an adverse gap (point 2), there is also an adverse breakpoint. This duplication deliberately results in double counting because of the high probability of failure when trading against adverse gaps—unless outweighed by favorable gaps or islands.

4. *Adverse Channel Line*: Occurs when price is near a channel line, as opposed to a trendline. (Channel lines are above the market in a bull market and below the market in a bear market.) Although price may surge through a channel line, the probabilities do not favor entering a trade at a channel line in the expectation of that happening.

5. *Double Top/Bottom*: Occurs when price is near a double top or bottom, generally one of more than seven weeks' standing. In the absence of extremely powerful action, the probabilities tend to favor price not following through. That is how range traders make their money.

6. *Adverse Trendline*: Occurs when price is near an important *downtrend* line when buying or an *uptrend* line when selling.

To determine the net confirming indicators, subtract the total negating indicators from the total confirming indicators. If there are five or more net confirming indicators on the weekly chart, the market is qualified to trade. In this case, go through the checklist on the daily chart.

Qualification on the weekly chart of a market to trade may occur some time before an entry is signaled on the daily list or simultaneously. The probabilities are seldom favorable for a major trade when the daily chart signals a trade without the market being qualified to trade on the weekly chart.

Form 2, Other Indicators

The other indicators on the entry checklist are somewhat more subjective and are therefore not added to the scoring. However, each has enough importance to tip the balance in making a trading decision when there is only the minimum of five net confirming indicators and one or more of the readings is ambiguous. When several of these other indicators strongly confirm or oppose an intended trade, believe them and act accordingly.

There is no set rule as to when to check the other indicators, although Form 2 provides for their review on the daily checklist, with the exception of on balance volume and accumulation/distribution. In practice, you might be aware of an imbalance in the Commitments of Traders numbers, and therefore of a potential major trade, many weeks before actually considering a trade. On the other hand, the 60-minute chart and the stop will likely be considered only when the net confirming indicators suggest an immediate entry.

1. *60-Minute Chart*: Sometimes the 60-minute chart shows a pattern that looks almost certain to follow through the next day, possibly with a stochastic/gap signal. In this case, factor it into the decision to trade, and possibly also the number of contracts to trade. Remember that a high made early in the day but not subsequently exceeded may be a warning that the market cannot follow through, even if the close is near the top of the day's range. The opposite applies to lows when considering a short position. Some of the best trades occur when the 60-minute chart has a steady staircase appearance in the direction of the intended trade.

2. *Commitments of Traders*: CoT can serve as an invaluable contrary indicator at extremes. Once you have started collecting a record for comparison, check whether the current weighting of traders suggests that the market is vulnerable to a sharp rebound, either for or against the proposed trade.

3. *On Balance Volume*: OBV is usually best at signaling price climaxes. Sometimes trend changes occur with a climactic bulge in OBV. A succession of three higher lows frequently indicates a current or an impending low in price; a declining triple top often signals a top in price.

4. *Accumulation/Distribution*: A/D performs best as a trend indicator. In established trends, A/D should more or less maintain a zigzag in the same direction as price. Watch for non-confirming zigzags as a sign of a possible trend change. A/D and OBV are most useful when they are both delivering the same message.

5. *Backwardation*: Also known as an inverted or a premium market, back-wardation occurs when the nearby contract is trading above the price of the deferred contracts because of a shortage of supply in *physical commodities* that

is expected to be alleviated later. Backwardation often occurs in the strongest bull markets and can remain in force for many months.

Backwardation frequently occurs in interest rates, currencies and the petroleum complex for various reasons. In these markets, backwardation should not be considered a signal of a major bull market. However, increasing backwardation in the petroleum complex normally indicates at least short-term tightness of supplies.

In inverted markets in physical commodities, buy the nearby contract. Prices are in backwardation because of intense immediate demand for insufficient supplies. Consequently, the price of the nearby contract will always rise more than that of the deferred contracts. There is normally no way of knowing how long the situation causing backwardation will last and thus whether the price of the deferred contracts will ever catch up with the price of the nearby contract.

Be very cautious about selling an inverted market short. Markets can top and start a bear trend while inverted. But if considering selling short, be sure that the indicators confirm a top and that backwardation has been steadily decreasing.

Aside from our regular indicators, one additional factor should be monitored when trading inverted markets: the spread among several contracts. If the spread starts to shrink, it suggests a changing supply and demand picture, and the possibility of a near-term or longer-term top. If the spread subsequently starts to expand again, it suggests that supply and demand remain unbalanced.

6. *Stop/Capital Management*: You can't trade without knowing where the stop is and how many contracts to trade, if any, according to the dictates of capital management (Chapter 15). Enter the stop at the same time as the entry order.

Timing Market Entry

The practicality of making real-time trading decisions quite often results in entry signals being identified after the market has closed. When an entry has been missed that should have been taken on the close, according to Five Star procedures, you can generally enter at an acceptable price on the open the next day.

Alternatively, you may see that a market has not quite completed an entry signal but is expected to do so. This situation frequently occurs at crests and valleys in strongly trending markets. In these cases, it can often be very effective to enter the market by placing a stop just beyond the previous day's high when buying, or just below the previous day's low when selling. The order is the same mechanism as is used for protective stops, except that you use it as the means to enter new trades.

Entering markets by stop is also useful when price is faltering at a support or resistance level and there is no way of knowing whether it can break through or not. The ambiguity of whether or not support or resistance can hold often results in substantial follow-through when it is resolved by a breakout: a lot of other traders are also waiting to know whether the breakout is going to occur.

Many traders believe that you should look for a good entry price after making the decision to enter a market. After much testing of the potential gains from saving on some entries versus the opportunity costs from failing to enter some markets because the designated price was not met, the conclusion is clear. The very best trades do not give you an opportunity to enter at a better price than is available when the signal is first delivered. Sometimes if you don't pull the trigger immediately, it becomes very difficult to do so subsequently, both psychologically and from the practical standpoint of a reasonable stop. It often seems that inferior trades will let you enter at a better price but many of the ones that turn into the megatrades that make futures trading truly worthwhile never look back.

Essentially, the higher the quality of a trade in terms of its technical picture, the more important it is to enter exactly when the signal to enter occurs. If the signal occurs in conjunction with a limit move or a major reversal, there is a high probability that there will be no better entry price than to trade into the limit before it jams, or into the close of the reversal day. The next best entry will likely be the open the next day, especially if there is a gap with the trend. That should draw more money into the trade.

If you absolutely insist on the pursuit of better entry prices—a psychological need for some people, the remedy is to enter a partial position when the signal occurs. Then you retain funds for the better-priced entry that you seek. The problem with this approach is that the best trades will probably not look back and it is those which deserve additional contracts, not the ones that retrace to a better entry price and possibly fade out altogether.

Chapter 19

Liquidating Trades

The purpose of trading futures is to make money. It is also to maximise profits to the greatest extent possible. However, there is an inherent contradiction in this objective. On the one hand, a trade has to be given room to move, particularly when it is making money and likely to make more. On the other hand, all retracements, regardless of whether the trade is making money or not, reduce the value of the account. There will always be trades liquidated too late because they were given too much room to move and gave back too much trading capital in the process. As well, there will always be trades liquidated too early because they were given too little room to move and were liquidated or stopped out immediately before going on to great things.

It is therefore important to understand that very few significant trading opportunities consist of only one ideal entry and one ideal exit. You should always be prepared to re-enter a market when it shows that it is likely to continue with its move. Although this sounds like common sense, it can be difficult to put into practice. Most traders are subject to psychological forces that make it easy to accept small losses or small adverse retracements in profitable trades and very difficult to accept larger retracements, even when they do no damage to the technical case for a trade. Quite often a trade that is liquidated after incurring a hefty loss or giving back a substantial profit is actually near a very favorable point for re-entry. This is because the market will have become quite overbought or oversold and will have finished washing out weak holders. Ability to re-enter the market at that point is a function of capital management and of psychology.

Given the inherent conflicts in liquidating trades, we have three approaches: catching problems early, taking profits on the basis of objectives, and liquidating trades on the basis of Five Star exit signals, for which we use Form 3.

Catching Problems Early

Ideally, a trade should quickly proceed to a profit if it has been entered with five or more net confirming Five Star indicators. If this does not occur, it may be for a variety of reasons. For example, aberrant, short-term price behavior may have caused the indicators to give misleading positive signals. Or the market may be marking time because it is waiting for certain events to occur, such as the release of statistical reports or other fundamental information.

For trades that look as if they may fail from the outset, go through the entry checklist again. If there are negating indicators in force and the number of net confirming indicators has fallen below five, it is probably better to exit immediately and wait for a new entry signal. Indicators such as %K and the four-price line turn as soon as they become negative. In the case of a price rule signal, assume that it remains in force until it is negated by a price rule signal to go the other way.

Profit-Taking by Objectives

When holding a trade that has done well, there is always a temptation to take too close to the heart the saying "Let your profits run!" But, based on Chapters 6, 8 and 9, we could add "Support and resistance levels work!" Even the best trades do come to an end. You should be prepared to take a profit when a market has reached a conspicuous target, instead of waiting to give back that portion of the profit that generates the exit signal (or, in the worst case, takes away all the profit or even turns it into a loss). Remember that very overbought or oversold markets can turn suddenly and violently.

Look for the following circumstances in which to take profits, rather than wait for an exit signal.

1. Price has reached a major barrier on the monthly, weekly and/or daily chart: an important adverse breakpoint (horizontal support or resistance, or a gap), a channel line or long-term adverse trendline, the most distant moving average or, on the daily chart, the contract high or low for both nearest futures and the month traded, if different.

    If you are expecting a market to break through a major support or resistance level, you may be right. But the probabilities favor the market taking a few runs at it first if, in fact, it is going to happen at all.

2. %K is conspicuously overbought or oversold on the weekly and/or daily chart. On the daily chart, %K seldom exceeds 80 or 20 for long without a significant retracement occurring. When %K is above 90 or below 10, the probabilities in favor of a continuation of price without a retracement are very low, except in the most rapidly moving markets.

3. A market that has been making limit moves stops trading at limit. Those traders compelled to cover will likely have finished doing so. Consequently, there is a high probability that the market has run out of fire-power to go further. A major trend change may occur after a series of limit moves has run its course.

4. The market has completed a measured move. The theory states that a market is likely to move from a breakout by an amount approximately equal to the distance it covered in its immediately preceding move. This approach is generally most applicable on the weekly chart but is also worth heeding on

the daily chart. It is quite reliable with bigger formations such as a head-and-shoulders pattern and a major triangle. It works best when the price objective coincides with an important support or resistance level, or other barrier. The best trades generally accelerate toward such barriers.

Depending on whether or not you can monitor the market during trading hours, the best way to protect profits when one or more of the above circumstances exists is to:

1. Exit at the market; or

2. Enter a tight stop; or

3. Exit on an adverse gap open; or

4. Use the 60-minute chart for fine-tuning an exit, especially in the event of an adverse price rule signal.

If you are trading multiple contracts, you have the flexibility to liquidate some of your positions when a target is reached, while retaining the balance until an outright exit signal occurs. When trading single contracts, it is generally preferable to liquidate at a major price objective.

Form 3, Confirming Indicators

The primary tool for liquidating trades is Form 3, Five Star Exit Checklist. It is the counterpart of the entry checklist and is completed in the same way. Reversing the procedure for entries, exit signals usually show up on the daily chart before they do on the weekly chart. Therefore, on Form 3 the indicators on the *daily* chart are far more important than those on the weekly chart. A review of the weekly indicators remains valuable though. Without it, you may not see that price is turning at an important barrier on the weekly chart, which is not apparent on the daily chart.

It takes a net total of five confirming daily indicators (confirming indicators minus negating ones) to liquidate a trade. When there is a net total of four confirming indicators on the daily chart, place a tight stop and exit quickly if adverse price action continues, particularly if there is an adverse gap on the next open.

As on the entry checklist, use a tick when an indicator confirms action, an X when it negates action and leave the space blank when it is not applicable.

1. *Four-Price Line*: Turns against the trade. It is particularly significant when the four-price line forms an M or a W against the trade, thereby suggesting the potential to break through support or resistance.

2. *Single-Price Line*: Turns against the trade.

3. *MACD*: Fast line turns against the trade. It is generally a strong warning of a potentially serious adverse retracement when the fast line crosses the slow one and moves in the opposite direction to the assumed price trend.

4. *%K Turn*: Turns against the trade.

5. *Adverse Price Rule Signal*: See Chapter 5 for the eight rules. An adverse price rule signal is the normal trigger for liquidating a trade when other indicators confirm an exit.

   The four-and single-price lines, MACD and %K frequently turn against a trade, even in a strongly trending market, as a result of a market consolidation rather than a more substantial retracement. Therefore, it is generally better to stay in a trade unless there is an adverse price rule signal to exit. Sometimes, however, a preponderance of other signals confirm liquidation and indicate that a trade should be exited without waiting for an adverse price rule signal.

6. *25-Bar Moving Average (MA) Direction*: Points in the opposite direction to the trade.

7. *40-Bar Moving Average (MA) Direction*: Points in the opposite direction to the trade.

8. *Adverse Trendline Close*: In a bear market, price closes on the top side of a downtrend line. In a bull market, price closes on the under side of an uptrend line.

9. *Adverse Double Reversal (Price Rule 8)*: Price closes in the adverse top or bottom 25 percent of the bars' ranges. This is a strong indication of a market's potential to change direction, at least in the near term. If it occurs when %K is overbought or oversold, there may be a substantial retracement. (This indicator is generally applicable only on the daily checklist.)

10. *Adverse Key Reversal (Price Rule 2)*: Price closes in the adverse top or bottom 25 percent of the bar's range. This shows a potential shift in buying or selling pressure sufficient to start a significant retracement. If an outside bar occurs in conjunction with an adverse double reversal, count each one separately, for a total of two.

11. *Adverse Gaps: Recent Total (Price Rule 3)*: Occur when there is a blank space between one bar and the next one or when price draws away from the close of the previous bar and fails to fill the gap on a closing basis. Count a separate tick for each gap within the most recent consolidation or formation, generally during the past week or so.

12. *Islands (Include 60-Minute Chart) (Price Rule 4)*: Occurs when there is blank space on the chart as a result of price first gapping up and then down, or vice versa. It also occurs when there is gapping away from closes first in one direction and then in the other, even if the ranges of two or more bars overlap.

    The more time taken to form an island and the more symmetrical it is, the more likely that there is an important turning point.

Form 3 Five Star EXIT Checklist

Contract:_____ Long:_____ Short:_____ Date Started: _____

	Weekly Chart						Daily Chart					
Confirming Indicators: Exit												
Date												
1. Four-Price Line												
2. Single-Price Line												
3. MACD												
4. % K Turn												
5. Adverse Price Rule Signal												
6. 25-Bar MA Direction												
7. 40-Bar MA Direction												
8. Adverse Trendline Close												
9. Adverse Double Reversal												
10. Adverse Key Reversal												
11. Adverse Gaps: Recent Total												
12. Islands (Include. 60-Min. Chart)												
13. %K Level [1]												
14. Adverse Weekly Reversal [2]												
15. At Support or Resistance [3]												
Total												
Negating Indicators: Stay												
1. Favorable Gap(s)												
2. Favorable Breakpoint Holding												
3. Favorable %K Level [1]												
4. Favorable Trendline Holding												
Total												
NET CONFIRMING INDICATORS (Confirming – Negating: 5 Needed) [4]												
Other Indicators												
1. 60-Minute Chart												
2. Commitments of Traders												
3. On Balance Volume												
4. Accumulation/Distribution												
5. Backwardation												
6. Stop/Capital Management												

[1] %K is overbought on the weekly chart at >80 and on the daily chart at >70. It is oversold on the weekly chart at <20 and on the daily chart at <30.

[2] Count on both the weekly and daily charts.

[3] Check the weekly and daily charts for double (or more) adverse tops or bottoms, adverse gaps or breakpoints, channel lines and long-term adverse trendlines, and the daily chart for contract high or low.

[4] When there is a net total of 4 confirming exit indicators on the daily chart, place a tight stop and exit quickly if adverse price action continues, particularly if there is an adverse gap on the next open.

Since an island occurs with a gap, count both points 11 and 12. If an island occurs only on the *daily* chart, also count it on the weekly chart. Also count islands on the 60-minute chart.

13. *%K Level*: On the *weekly* chart, %K is or has recently been at or above 80, if long, or at or below 20, if short.

    On the *daily* chart, %K is or has recently been at or above 70, if long, or at or below 30, if short.

    The negative implications of an overbought or oversold %K level have to be tempered with the recognition that the most powerful moves result in extreme stochastics readings very early in the move. The %K level may therefore suggest an exit much too early and long before other indicators confirm it.

14. *Adverse Weekly Reversal*: Counts on both the weekly and daily charts, regardless of whether a price rule signal also occurs. Any closing price or key reversal counts, even when the close is not in the adverse 25 percent of the bar's range.

    Valid high/low reversals are more subjective to identify because of the potential for variation in extent and positioning of the second bar versus the first. Therefore, in the case of a high/low reversal, the last bar should close in the adverse 25 percent of its range to count.

15. *At Support or Resistance*: Price has reached a major barrier: an important adverse breakpoint (horizontal support or resistance, or a gap), a channel line or long-term adverse trendline, the most distant moving average or, on the daily chart, the contract high or low for both the nearest futures and the month traded, if different.

    If price is at or near a level of support or resistance on the monthly or weekly chart, it applies also to the daily chart, even when the action occurred too far back to be seen on the daily chart. In this case, count on both the weekly and daily charts. It is important to look carefully for long-standing support and resistance because it can be easy to overlook.

    This point was also described in a preceding section on profit-taking by objectives.

Form 3, Negating Indicators

Negating indicators on the exit form are indicators that suggest *staying with* a trade. They are therefore subtracted from the number of indicators signaling liquidation of a trade.

1. *Favorable Gap(s)*: Gaps in the direction of the trend suggest runaway buying or selling pressure. However, it is normal for a market to come back to test into a gap before continuing in the direction of the trend. A gap is negated by

being filled on a closing basis or by a gap in the opposite direction, thereby creating an island.

2. *Favorable Breakpoint Holding*: This indicator supports staying in a trade when the market has already retraced to an important support level for a long position or to an important resistance level for a short position.

   A breakpoint includes: horizontal support or resistance, a gap or a prominent price spike that acts as support or resistance. Because a gap (point 1) is also a breakpoint, there may be a tick for each of them.

3. *Favorable %K Level*: Occasionally an exit may be considered when a trade on the long side is already oversold, according to the %K reading, or a trade on the short side is overbought. In a strong bull market, %K on the daily chart seldom goes below 30, and if it does, the market is more likely to be a buy than a sell. In a strong bear market, the corresponding number is 70.

4. *Favorable Trendline Holding*: If a retracement results in price pressing against an uptrend line in a bull market or a downtrend line in a bear market, there is a high probability of the trendline holding, at least on a closing basis.

   When a market is trending strongly and both the 25- and 40-day moving averages are clearly pointing in the direction of a trend, be prepared to err on the side of staying in a trade, rather than liquidating it if there is not a clear exit signal. A market will often close at the adverse extremity of a daily range against a trendline and reverse the next day in the direction of the trend. Therefore, in such a case it is often appropriate to wait one more day, or at least until the open of the next day's trading, if the trend is strong and especially if the trade shows a profit.

Form 3, Other Indicators

As on the entry checklist, the exit checklist provides for considering other indicators that are somewhat more subjective and are therefore not included in the scoring. However, it can be very valuable to review these indicators when a decision to liquidate is ambiguous. It is particularly useful to be aware of large bulges in on balance volume but to have confidence in the ability of a trend to continue when accumulation/distribution is moving steadily in the direction of the trend. Triple tops and triple bottoms in either OBV or in A/D often occur in conjunction with at least intermediate trend changes.

If you have access to 60-minute intraday charts, you can often see a market setting up the day before an adverse move, just as you can see it setting up for a potential trend continuation. It is always worth looking at the 60-minute chart at the end of the day to see whether the market has lined up for a potential gap or an adverse continuation against your trade. This may be the tip-off for action to exit a market if there are not yet five indicators confirming an exit.

Finally, when you liquidate a trade, don't forget to cancel the stop!

You may notice an apparent anomaly on the exit checklist regarding trendlines. A trendline holding is an indicator to stay in a trade but there is no confirming indicator to exit for an adverse trendline crossover. We find that pressure at or near a trendline, even an adverse close, is more likely to be favorable for adding contracts or entering new positions than for exiting, unless other indicators signal an exit. This is because a short position pressing against a downtrend line, or even going slightly through it, may be somewhat overbought and at or near the extremity of a retracement (and vice versa for a long position pressing against an uptrend line). Therefore, the signal to liquidate or to stay pivots on the overall action of the indicators.

Exits are normally signaled first on the daily checklist. However, it is often useful to go through the weekly exit checklist despite the fact that doing so may seem superfluous. Sometimes it shows that you simply shouldn't be in a trade at all. In that case, it is probably best to liquidate immediately, rather than assume that the weekly chart will come on side. Even under the best of circumstances, it may mean a long wait.

It is appropriate that a trading system devote more attention to entries than to exits. The biggest and best trades need looking for. Once found, trades well entered in prime markets to trade are likely to be a good source of profits. They are the equivalent for futures traders of the retailer's saying that merchandise well bought is already half sold. However, an approach to trading that does not also keep a constant eye on the exit can decimate or destroy those profits that have been so carefully sought out.

The next section summarises the prime liquidation signals. As for the top Five Star entry indicators in Chapter 16, we have put them on a separate page so that you may easily copy and post them as a reminder when considering whether to retain or to liquidate a trade.

Prime Liquidation Signals

It is all too easy to liquidate a good trade prematurely, and all too tempting to do so when there is a big profit. Despite this caution, when two or more of the following conditions occur, go through Form 3, the exit checklist with particular care and be prepared to liquidate quickly or immediately. This list is relatively long because exits can be difficult.

1. Price has reached a conspicuous support or resistance level on the monthly and/or weekly chart.

   Be sure to refer to the monthly chart as well as the weekly chart when trading a major market move that takes price to a very high or a very low historic level.

2. Price has reached an adverse gap or island on the daily chart.

   Adverse gaps and islands are very likely to act as an impenetrable barrier, particularly on the first one or two assaults. Remember the saying "Support and resistance levels work!"

3. Price has reached a channel line on the daily chart or, even more important, on the weekly chart.

4. %K on the weekly chart is overbought or oversold (>80, <20).

5. %K on the daily chart makes an M or a W at an overbought or oversold level (>70, <30).

6. The market requires less steep trendlines on the daily and/or weekly chart.

   This situation is easily overlooked when entering a trade. If it is recognized after entry, the case for being in the trade may be suspect. The decreasing steepness of trendlines often shows up first on the 60-minute chart.

7. The weekly chart pattern fails to confirm the trade.

   A trade can be entered in anticipation of some weekly chart indicators turning in support of a trade. If they fail to confirm, the market may be completing a retracement prior to moving in the opposite direction to the trade or it may be going into a trading range.

8. The trade has not gone to a profit five days after entry.

   Such a trade has to be called into question. Redo the entry checklist to see whether the case for the trade still holds. Also complete the exit checklist.

Finally, remember that liquidating a trade does not necessarily mean the end of trading a particular market. The best markets to trade will likely have several entries and exits.

Chapter 20

Case Study: Established Trend

This chapter and the following three chapters bring together all the preceding material by applying it in a real-time manner, as you would if faced with trading decisions on a day-to-day basis. Chapters 20 to 22 examine trades in each of the three kinds of market action that the Five Star system seeks to trade: established trends, rapidly moving markets and major trend changes. This chapter contains more detail than the subsequent two, including the point-by-point completion of Form 2, the entry checklist.

Prime Entry Indicators

By January 1994 the Canadian Dollar had been in a bear market for over three years, since November 1991 (Chart 20.1a). In late 1993 it had declined to an important support area on the monthly chart and then rallied four cents. The question therefore was: Would the established bear trend in the Canadian Dollar continue? We can see in hindsight that it did. But cover the area to the right of the weekly chart from mid-January 1994 and put yourself in the position of making trading decisions on the basis of the evidence as it unfolded.

To try to determine what the Canadian Dollar might be doing, we reviewed the prime entry indicators for markets in established trends on the weekly Canadian Dollar chart as of the week ending January 21, 1994. Each of the points below refers to the relevant prime entry indicators, as described in Chapter 16.

1. The four-price line showed a steady pattern of lower highs and lower lows but the December 1994 low was slightly above the one in October. The December rally could either be the start of a new trend or the market could be setting up to fall through the bottom of a descending triangle.

2. MACD was showing bullish divergence. It had a higher low in October 1993 and the fast line had crossed to the upside of the slow line, suggesting that the end of the bear market could be approaching. MACD is a very early indicator of a major trend change.

3.   %K was at a neutral reading of 53, well below the level of 64 reached in November 1993. If it turned down under 64, it would be bearish.

4.   The 25- and 40-week moving averages were pointing strongly down and price remained below the 40-week average, although it had gone through the 25-week average several times. The moving averages suggested that the market had gotten ahead of itself at the October low and that recent sideways action was merely allowing the moving averages to catch up with the price.

5.   The major long-term trendline from the 1991 high had been penetrated by the rally in October and November, and slightly by the retracement in January. However, a somewhat flatter trendline from the highs in March and May 1993 had contained all rallies, including the peak in November. Price action against the trendlines did not suggest that the bear market was finished.

6.   The December low on the daily chart established a seven-week low, thereby confirming the big picture for a bear market. However, the high for the week ending January 21 was a new seven-week high.

7.   Price closed near its high for the week, at the flattest downtrend line and near the downtrending 40-week moving average.

The review of the prime entry indicators for markets in an established trend suggested that the Canadian Dollar should be watched closely. It seemed likely that a signal indicating resumption of the bear trend could occur soon.

Forms 1 and 2

The next trading day, Monday, January 24, we reviewed the daily Canadian Dollar on Form 1, Five Star Daily Market Checklist (Charts 20.2a and b). %K was at 81. Price had done a small daily downside reversal and was potentially also turning back down at the trendline on the weekly chart. We therefore checked the weekly indicators on Form 2, Five Star Entry Checklist, to determine whether the Canadian Dollar was giving signs of possibly resuming its bear trend and was thus shaping up for a short sale. The results merely confirmed that this was a market to watch. Because it had rallied so strongly, it was logical to assume that it might take some time to complete its upward thrust. Consequently, we continued to check the indicators on the *weekly* portion of Form 2 every day.

Weekly Confirming Indicators

By Thursday, January 27 a weekly downside reversal at the 40-week moving average and flattest downtrend line looked probable. The status of the confirming indicators on the weekly Canadian Dollar chart (Charts 20.1a and b) is shown on completed Form 2, page 141 and described below. We analyse markets before the close in order to enter by the close if the signals confirm a trade. Those unable to do this work intraday can do it after hours to determine what action should be taken the next day, normally on the open.

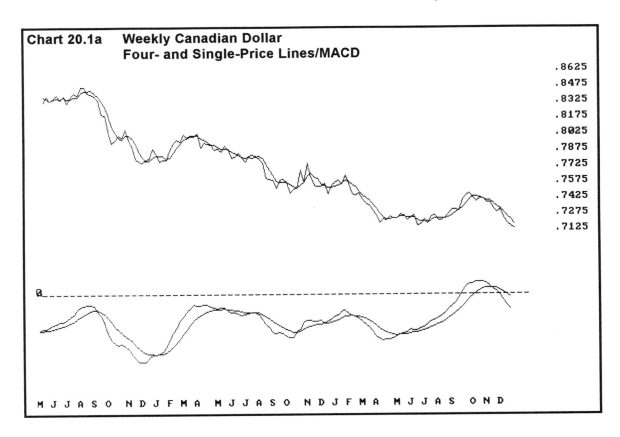

Chart 20.1a   Weekly Canadian Dollar
Four- and Single-Price Lines/MACD

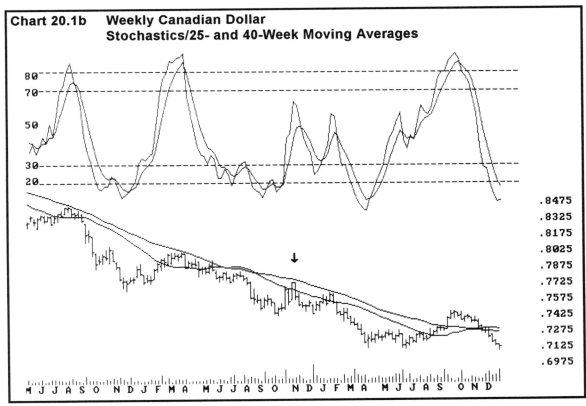

Chart 20.1b   Weekly Canadian Dollar
Stochastics/25- and 40-Week Moving Averages

1.   Four-Price Line: No downturn evident yet. Count 0.

2.   Single-Price Line: Downturn. Count 1.

3.   MACD: No downturn. Count 0.

4.   % K Turn: No downturn. Count 0.

5.   25-Week Moving Average: Pointing strongly down. Count 1.

6.   40-Week Moving Average: Pointing strongly down. Count 1.

7.   Price Rule Signal: A potential high/low reversal, which cannot be confirmed until the next day's close. Not tremendously convincing on the weekly chart but the daily price action is bearish enough to assume the signal. Count 1.

8.   Reversal at Moving Average/Trendline: There was one close above the 25-week moving average but none above the 40-week. The likely reversal here would provide one of the strongest indications of the market's potential to resume its bear market trend. Count 1.

9.   Outside Bar: Not applicable. Count 0.

10.   Double Reversal: There was a kind of downside reversal two weeks earlier but it is too unclear to count, especially in view of the market's current higher price and the pre-emptive situation regarding the current bar. Count 0.

11.   Gap: The nearby contract closed last week at .7621 and opened on Monday at .7608, a downward gap of 13 points. Although the market rallied back through the weekly unchanged price, it could not hold there. Therefore, count 1.

12.   Island: There was a weekly gap down on the open this week; the previous week there was a gap up on the open. For our purposes, we count this action as an island unless the gap down open is filled on a weekly closing basis. Count 1.

There were seven confirming indicators on the weekly checklist, two more than the minimum required to continue with an analysis of the negating indicators.

Weekly Negating Indicators

1.   % K Level: With a reading of 57, % K should be nearer a top than a bottom. It would take a reading of 20 or lower to count negatively. Count 0.

2.   Adverse Gap(s): There is an unfilled gap under the market at .7540, the close for the week of January 14, from which price gapped up on the open of the next week. Count 1.

3.   Adverse Breakpoint(s): The close of the week ending January 14 is a break-point standing in the way of a further downside move but it could give way if there is enough pressure. Count 1.

4.   Adverse Channel Line: Not applicable. Count 0.

5. Double Top/Bottom: The double top is not applicable since we are looking to sell, not buy.   Count 0.

6. Adverse Trendline: Not applicable. (The downtrend line would count against the case for a trade only if we were looking to buy.) Count 0.

Two indicators negate the Canadian Dollar as a market qualified to sell short. But seven indicators confirm it, for a net total of five weekly confirming indicators, the exact minimum number required to qualify. Consequently, it is appropriate to examine the June Canadian Dollar chart (Charts 20.2a and b) and the daily column on the entry checklist for signals to enter a trade on the short side. (The June chart is used here for convenience as the period discussed is from January to April.)

Daily Confirming Indicators

1. Four-Price Line: Turned down on January 25, giving a sell signal. Count 1.

2. Single-Price Line: Turned down on January 20 and has remained down since. Count 1.

3. MACD: Turned down on January 25. Count 1.

4. %K Turn: Turned down on January 25 from 81, a very high level. Count 1.

5. 25-Day Moving Average: Pointing up, not down. Count 0.

6. 40-Day Moving Average: Pointing up, not down. Count 0.

7. Price Rule Signal: A rule 5, Lindahl sell signal plus a rule 8, double reversal signal. Count 1.

8. Reversal at Moving Averages/Trendline: Not applicable. Count 0.

9. Outside Bar: Not applicable. Count 0.

10. Double Reversal: There was a downside closing price reversal on January 24 and a second one on January 27. Count 1.

11. Gap: The market gapped down on January 26 versus the close of the previous day. Despite the big upward thrust on January 27, that gap was not filled on a closing basis and remains in force. Count 1.

12. Island: There was an island in the making with the gap down on January 26. However, the upward thrust on January 27 and the erratic market action suggest that an island should not be counted. Count 0.

Seven indicators confirm entry into a new short position. Therefore, the negating indicators are examined next.

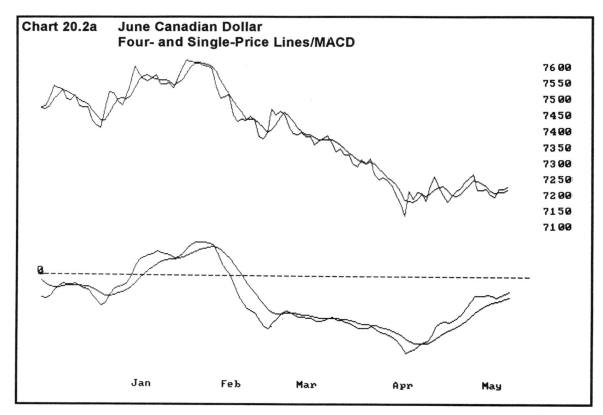

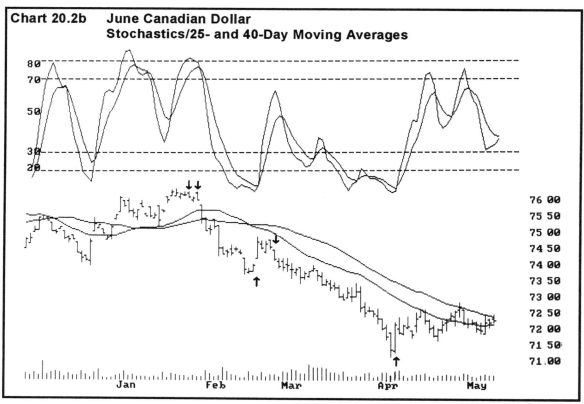

Daily Negating Indicators

1. % K Level: Reached 81, a very overbought level rather than an oversold level (30 or lower), which would count against the trade. Count 0.

2. Adverse Gap(s): There was a gap up from a close on January 18 at .7596. Subsequent market action suggested that it was an exhaustion gap but until it is filled on a closing basis, it counts against the trade. There was another adverse gap under the market from the close on January 17 at .7564. We decide not to count it because price action strongly suggests a significant top, and the gap is sufficiently below the current price to allow it to be tested and a profit or a breakeven trade to be booked if the gap supports price. Count one against the trade, rather than the potential two adverse points, but pay particular attention to other indicators such as Commitments of Traders to tip the balance, if necessary.

3. Adverse Breakpoint: The adverse gap (point 2) also counts as a support level that could stop the market's decline. The double-counting is intentional because of the importance of potential adverse support (or resistance). Count 1.

4. Adverse Channel Line: Not applicable. Count 0.

5. Double Top/Bottom: This would be a negating indicator only when selling low in the expectation of a double bottom giving way. Instead, we expect the double top to hold. Count 0.

6. Adverse Trendline: Not applicable. Count 0.

The results of doing the daily entry checklist for Thursday, January 27 are seven confirming indicators minus two negating indicators, for a net total of five, the minimum required for a potential trade. We therefore proceed to the other indicators to consider whether any of these factors might tip the balance for or against the trade.

Other Indicators

1. 60-Minute Chart: With the close right at the bottom of the daily range, the probability of the market following through and possibly gapping down the next day is excellent. If a gap occurs, it would be at the same level as the previous gap, thereby establishing an eight-day island, which would cancel the two negating indicators on the daily checklist.

2. Commitments of Traders: The data for January 17 showed:

    a) non-commercials were net long 17 percent, down from net long 26 percent on January 4;

    b) commercials were net short 39 percent, up from net short 37 percent on January 4; and

    c) small traders were net long 22 percent, up from net long 10 percent.

1. On Balance Volume: There were lower major highs on January 3 and 19. The low on January 26 was lower than the January 14 low. OBV definitely shows a distribution pattern.

2. Accumulation/Distribution: Shows an extremely pronounced bearish pattern.

3. Backwardation: The nearby contract is priced slightly above the deferred. This differential is normal when traders expect a currency to decline over the longer term. Backwardation in the currencies is somewhat bearish, rather than bullish as it is for physical commodities.

4. Stop/Capital Management: The logical chart point stop is slightly above the high of the formation at .7630, say at .7643 in order to be above the round number. An entry at .7598 must budget for a potential loss of $450 in terms of the stop. As discussed in Chapter 9, there would probably be a lower risk of the market reversing if it gapped down on the open of January 28 and followed through, although the dollar amount of the stop would increase.

The action of the various indicators suggests that the Canadian Dollar on January 27 is about to resume its established bear trend. We therefore sell the market short on the close.

On January 28 the market gaps down on the open, as we foresaw could occur from the low close on January 27 in the area of a previous gap. The recent %K turn down from 81 and the gap open produce a classic stochastic/gap sell signal (discussed in Chapter 12). We therefore sell additional contracts short on the open.

It would also be valid to add contracts on the close on Friday, January 28 because a weekly downside reversal and many other weekly signals were confirming. Also, the eight-day island on the daily chart provided further support for adding contracts, even though the market had already moved some distance from its high. New entries should always be considered when an island appears at potential market crests in an established bear market (and at potential market bottoms in an established bull market).

As the completed Form 2 indicates, the entry checklist for January 28 requires some minor differences in interpretation. The double reversal confirming indicator no longer counts because it has become too distant to be relevant. Only one gap is counted because each gap inevitably takes price closer to its destination. However, a new confirming point is counted as a result of the formation of an island.

Two negating indicators are retained, one each for an adverse gap and an adverse breakpoint, which would now refer to the potential for support from the January 14 close at .7533. The market tested through that support level but failed to close below it on January 28.

Liquidation

Unless a trade is liquidated pre-emptively, as discussed in Chapter 19, or stopped out, the process for liquidating a trade is much the same as for entering, only in reverse. Once the trade was entered on January 27 and 28, we monitored it every day, using the daily market checklist. By February 9, %K was at 10, an extremely low level, and price was at .7435. A low %K reading, of itself, only sets up an alert for the possibility of a retracement. At that point, price action did not suggest that a low had been made. By February 15, %K was at 9, while price had declined considerably, to .7377. When %K turned up the next day and price failed to follow through with a low close for a third consecutive day, it seemed possible that a rally could start.

The stop for February 15 was therefore based on stop rule 6, rapidly moving markets without limits, which suggests that the stop be based on a logical chart point on the 60-minute chart. Given the gap down on February 14, the logical chart point on both the 60-minute and daily charts was the February 13 close at .7434.

On February 17 the market gapped up and opened at .7419, giving a classic stochastic/gap signal. The fact that the gap was as much as 23 points increased the probability of the market continuing in the direction of the gap as a violent reaction to a deeply oversold condition. This is exactly the kind of market action that can result in a major short-covering rally, as traders excessively weighted on the short side scramble for cover and the rally feeds on itself. We were quickly stopped out.

It is possible, however, that you might have decided that it was reasonable to live through all but the most ferocious short-covering rally in view of the apparent persistence of the bear market. For illustration, therefore, we assume that our position was not stopped out or exited prior to the close on February 17. Now we have to decide what to do about it, which leads to Form 3, Five Star Exit Checklist.

Form 3, Exit Checklist

The case for regarding the Canadian Dollar as being in a major bear market sustained little damage as a result of the retracement on February 17. The most important indicator to note is the weekly upside reversal, potentially a key reversal (which would have been caught in the making by the daily market checklist). When a market is overbought or oversold, weekly reversals so often lead to significant retracements that sensible capital management requires action to protect profits and/or trading capital.

An analysis of the weekly exit checklist shows a net score of only four confirming indicators (see completed Form 3, page 142). However, the *daily* exit checklist is, as with entries, the primary tool for signaling an actual exit. The indicators on the daily exit checklist almost universally confirm liquidation, with the island being the most notable of the confirming signals. If an island occurs on the wrong side of a trade, it is impossible to know how far or how fast the adverse move might go: islands frequently provide a powerful signal for trading in the direction of the new gapping.

There are no negating indicators to suggest staying in the market. Because there are no readily identifiable resistance levels nor a meaningful trendline, the market could rally all the way back toward the .7600 breakdown level. Therefore, liquidation is mandatory, with a total of nine indicators confirming liquidation and no negating ones to offset them.

Subsequent Action

The daily market checklist for February 23 indicated that the Canadian Dollar warranted further attention for a potential short sale. Although the weekly exit checklist the previous week showed only four indicators supporting a short position, this is a good example of how the picture can change quickly, with no need to wait until the close on Friday to act. Among the indicators that had moved offside were the single-price line and the price rule signal. But a new short sale could be confirmed if the single-price line went below the previous week's close at .7449 and the important price rule signal showed a weekly downside reversal (see Form 2).

On February 24, the market gapped down on the open. Therefore, you could make a pre-emptive short sale on the open or soon after it, or wait until the close for confirmation of the trade. As Form 2 indicates, it was confirmed on the close.

Liquidation of this trade would be handled in much the same way as the first one. For the week ending April 1, the weekly %K reading declined to an almost unprecedented 5, lower than at any time in the previous five years. Also, price was pressing against the lower side of a narrow channel that had been in effect for two months. %K on the daily chart was at 8, although price action did not suggest that the low had been reached.

On April 4, %K on the daily chart turned up to 9, although price fell by a further 39 points on the day. However, price failed to close near the bottom of its range, which is why %K was able to turn higher. As at the low in February, there was a fairly high probability that %K had just made a double bottom. The probabilities strongly suggested that this was a market that required either a pre-emptive liquidation or a tight stop at say .7194, or slightly above the April 4 high. Once adverse price action started on April 5, liquidation during the day would have been clearly called for, rather than waiting for the stop to be hit.

If you did not exit during the day and did not enter a stop within the range of trading for April 5, then you would go through the exit checklist. As Form 3 shows, the result is a conclusive signal to liquidate, with seven indicators confirming the exit and none negating it.

During the course of the second trade, there was just one other day when liquidation had to be considered, March 9. There was an adverse gap that broke clean away from the range for the previous day. However, price merely tested the downtrend line and the breakdown level from the close at .7397 on March 1.

The step-by-step procedures described in this chapter should provide you with a good basis for undertaking chart analyses on your own, using the daily market, entry and exit checklists. Chapters 21 to 23 therefore focus on identifying the prime indicators for a major trend change, a rapidly moving market and a vacuum crash.

Form 2   Five Star ENTRY Checklist

Contract: **CDM '94**   Buy:_____   Sell: ✓   Date Started: **1/27/94**

	Weekly Chart					Daily Chart				
Confirming Indicators										
Date	1/27	1/28		2/23	2/24	1/27	1/28		2/24	
1. Four-Price Line	X	✓		✓	✓	✓	✓		✓	
2. Single-Price Line	✓	✓		X	✓	✓	✓		✓	
3. MACD	X	X		✓	✓	✓	✓		✓	
4. % K Turn	X	✓		X	✓	✓	✓		✓	
5. 25- Bar MA Direction	✓	✓		X	✓	X	X		✓	
6. 40-Bar MA Direction	✓	✓		✓	✓	X	X		✓	
7. Price Rule Signal	✓	✓		✓	✓	✓	✓		✓	
8. Reversal at MA/Trendline	✓	✓			✓					
9. Key Reversal										
10. Double Reversal						✓				
11. Gap	✓	✓				✓	✓		✓	
12. Island [1]	✓	✓					✓		✓	
Total	7	9		4	8	7	7		9	
Negating Indicators										
1. Adverse %K Level [2]										
2. Adverse Gap(s) [3]	✓ ①	✓ ①				✓ ②	✓ ①		✓ ①	
3. Adverse Breakpoint	✓	✓				✓	✓		✓	
4. Adverse Channel Line										
5. Double Top/Bottom										
6. Adverse Trendline										
Total	2	2			0	2	2		2	
NET CONFIRMING INDICATORS (Confirming – Negating: 5 needed on both weekly & daily for entry)[4]	5	7			8	5	5		7	
Other Indicators										
1. 60-Minute Chart						✓	✓		✓	
2. Commitments of Traders						✓	✓		✓	
3. On Balance Volume	X	X			X	✓	✓		✓	
4. Accumulation/Distribution	X	X			X	✓	✓		✓	
5. Backwardation										
6. Stop/Capital Management						✓	✓		✓	

[1] If an island occurs only on the *daily* chart, also count it on the *weekly* chart.

[2] If %K is >80 or <20 on the weekly chart and/or >70 or <30 on the daily chart, count as a negating indicator.

[3] Enter one check for each adverse gap that remains unfilled on a closing basis during the most recent consolidation.

[4] For a potential *major trend change*, confirming indicators 1, 2, 3, 4 and 7 on the weekly and daily charts should confirm.

Form 3   Five Star EXIT Checklist

Contract: **CDM '94** Long:_____ Short: **✔** Date Started: **2/17/94**

	Weekly Chart				Daily Chart				
Confirming Indicators: Exit									
Date	2/17	4/1			2/17	4/5			
1. Four-Price Line	X	X			✔	X			
2. Single-Price Line	✔	X			✔	✔			
3. MACD	X	X			✔	✔			
4. % K Turn	✔	X			✔	✔			
5. Adverse Price Rule Signal	✔	X			✔	✔			
6. 25-Bar MA Direction	X	X			X	X			
7. 40-Bar MA Direction	X	X			X	X			
8. Adverse Trendline Close		X							
9. Adverse Double Reversal									
10. Adverse Key Reversal									
11. Adverse Gaps: Recent Total					✔ ①				
12. Islands (Include. 60-Min. Chart)					✔				
13. %K Level [1]		✔			✔	✔			
14. Adverse Weekly Reversal [2]	✔				✔	✔			
15. At Support or Resistance [3]		✔			✔				
Total	4	2			9	7			
Negating Indicators: Stay									
1. Favorable Gap(s)									
2. Favorable Breakpoint Holding									
3. Favorable %K Level [1]									
4. Favorable Trendline Holding									
Total					0	0			
NET CONFIRMING INDICATORS (Confirming – Negating: 5 Needed) [4]					9	7			
Other Indicators									
1. 60-Minute Chart					✔	✔			
2. Commitments of Traders					X	✔			
3. On Balance Volume					X	X			
4. Accumulation/Distribution					X	X			
5. Backwardation									
6. Stop/Capital Management					✔	✔			

[1] %K is overbought on the weekly chart at >80 and on the daily chart at >70. It is oversold on the weekly chart at <20 and on the daily chart at <30.

[2] Count on both the weekly and daily charts.

[3] Check the weekly and daily charts for double (or more) adverse tops or bottoms, adverse gaps or breakpoints, channel lines and long-term adverse trendlines, and the daily chart for contract high or low.

[4] When there is a net total of 4 confirming exit indicators on the daily chart, place a tight stop and exit quickly if adverse price action continues, particularly if there is an adverse gap on the next open.

Chapter 21

Case Study: Rapidly Moving Market

This chapter examines the second type of market that the Five Star system seeks to trade—rapidly moving markets—by describing a classic example, the enormous bull move by the Japanese Yen in early 1995.

Form 2, Weekly Chart Indicators

Until it broke up out of an eight-month consolidation, many people thought that the Japanese Yen could go in only one direction—down. But an analysis of this market for the period from late December 1994 to the end of February 1995, using Form 2, the entry checklist on the weekly chart, suggested the reverse.

The four-price line showed a prolonged rounding with an upward bias, and exceeded its previous high on February 24 (Chart 21.1a). The single-price line formed a bullishly skewed W. MACD bottomed and turned up, with its fast line crossing its slow line, thereby confirming the turn, on February 24. %K had been to 15 in early January and had turned sharply up (Chart 21.1b) . The 25-and 40-week moving averages continued to move slowly up. A price rule 5, Lindahl buy signal was delivered on February 10.

Commitments of Traders for February 14 showed both the non-commercials and the small traders heavily net short. OBV had formed a clear double bottom by late February. A/D broke out to a new high on February 17 after forming what had previously looked like a triple top.

In sum, all our indicators on the weekly chart, except one, had given buy signals by February 24. The only negating indicator was an adverse breakpoint, the double top of the long consolidation. For this discussion, though, we assume that an entry long was not made until the breakout occurred.

Prime Entry Indicators

On March 2 a major upside key reversal took price through the contract high at 106.15 (Chart 21.2b) and the weekly chart high at 104.42 (Chart 21.1b). The weekly chart indicated that the Yen had been in a bull market since 1990. Was the breakout to a new high simply the continuation of the established trend or was it possibly the first day of a rapidly moving market? A review of the prime entry indicators for rapidly moving markets (described in Chapter 16, page 105) would have provided the following answers.

1.   Both the weekly and daily chart for the Japanese Yen showed clear rounding or an emerging saucer from a left rim in November. (The June chart is shown only after the upward rounding started in order to provide more detail during the weeks when the market was moving.)

2.   The upside key reversal on March 2 was a strong breakout from a long consolidation. The range that day of 219 points far exceeded any recent action and the close near the top strongly suggested that it was unlikely to be a bull trap.

3.   With the market breaking to a new all-time high on the weekly chart, there was no overhead resistance.

4.   A new contract high was made on the daily chart. Therefore, every holder of a short position was a potential buyer to add fuel to the thrust, while every holder of a long position was building a cushion by adding contracts.

5.   There had been upward gaps on the June chart prior to the breakout but they were no more than early signs of the market's potential to move up. A gap did not occur on the day of the breakout.

The prime entry indicators for a rapidly moving market strongly suggested that the Yen was in the process of becoming such a market on March 2. Given this appraisal, entry checklist confirmation (see Charts 21.2a and b, and completed Form 2, page 150) and the powerful intraday action, it would be appropriate to enter the market during the day or on the close on March 2 or, if missed, on the next open. The initial protective stop, based on stop rule 6b, markets without limits, would be placed under the March 2 low of 104.31 at, say, 104.20.

Trading the Japanese Yen

As the daily Japanese Yen chart shows, waiting for a retracement of a market that has begun to move rapidly, rather than acting on an entry signal when it is given, can mean forgoing profits, increasing risk or missing the trade because the risk has become unmanageable. In the case of the Yen, a later initial entry would have increased the proximity of the entry price to the powerful 329-point downside reversal on March 8. For many traders with a relatively small profit cushion, this action would be stressful and could result in the trade being prematurely liquidated. But the reversal would have been relatively easy to tolerate for trades entered when the signal was given.

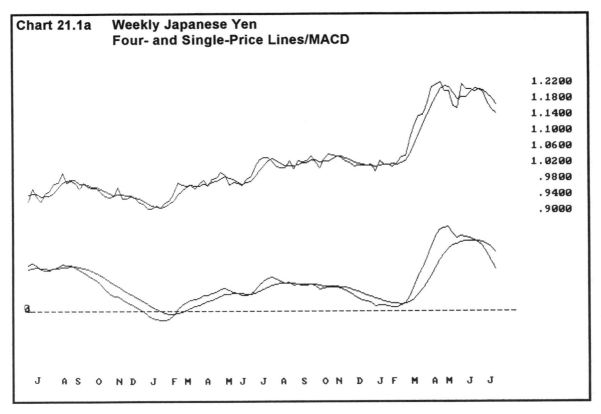

**Chart 21.1a   Weekly Japanese Yen
Four- and Single-Price Lines/MACD**

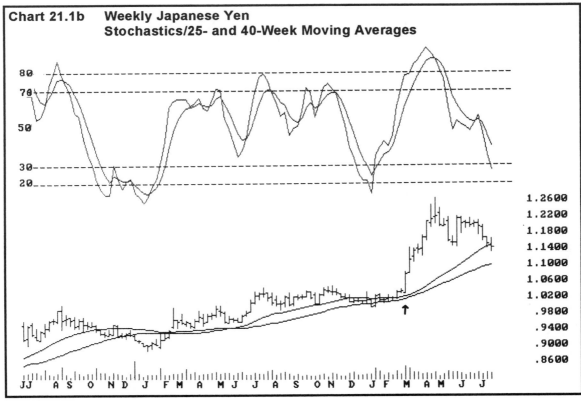

**Chart 21.1b   Weekly Japanese Yen
Stochastics/25- and 40-Week Moving Averages**

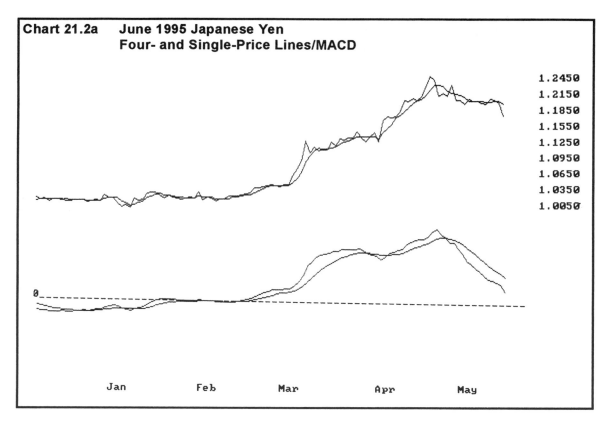

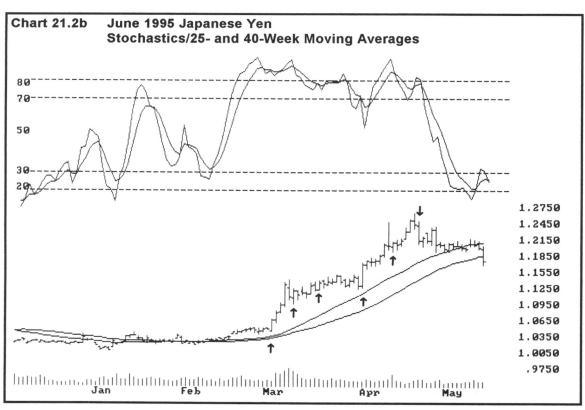

Downside reversals often occur in rapidly moving bull markets and upside reversals in rapidly moving bear markets because some traders like to lock in profits quickly. Although tops and bottoms often occur with adverse reversal days, there are far more adverse reversal days than market tops and bottoms. One adverse reversal day is likely to be no more than profit-taking, unless accompanied by other indications of a potential market turn.

The downside reversal on March 8, despite its big range, barely affected the confirming indicators on the daily chart. Consequently, the upside reversal the next day, March 9, produced a new entry signal, although it was not as strong as the initial entry signal. Because %K turned down, there was some possibility that the market might have to consolidate, possibly with a downward bias, before being able to move higher.

A third entry signal occurred on the close of March 17, when it looked as if the market could continue sharply higher. The entry checklist identified eight confirming indicators and one negating indicator, an overbought %K. However, the market did not immediately follow through and adverse price action led to the exit checklist being completed on March 27 (see completed Form 3, page 151). Seven indicators confirmed liquidation and two negated it, for a net total of five confirming indicators.

Because only the minimum number of indicators confirmed liquidation in an apparently strong rapidly moving market, these indicators were examined further to see how negative they actually were. For example, the adverse price rule signal was activated by a close barely in the bottom 25 percent of the day's range. The adverse gap signal resulted from a one point difference between the open of March 24 and the close of March 23.

On the other hand, both OBV and A/D, for example, strongly confirmed the underlying buying power in the market. Also, the weekly chart showed no sign of the market being ready to reverse, although it might need to consolidate. Therefore, it was decided that no damage would be done to the case for a continuing bull market unless price broke down out of its recent range to where the stop was placed at 1.1176, 10 points below the logical chart point on March 17, based on the gap up open. If you did liquidate on the close of March 27, you might have re-entered by stop above the high of 1.1452 on March 30, say at 1.1467.

The action on March 31 was a classic upside breakout from a consolidation that had lasted just over three weeks. Seven indicators on the entry checklist confirmed a new buy and only one, an overbought %K, negated it. Given the very high probability of powerful breakouts from consolidations in a rapidly moving market to follow through, this was an excellent place for either an initial entry or for adding contracts.

It can be psychologically difficult to enter a new trade when the market has already moved a huge amount in a single day—in this case 392 points, worth $4,900. However, such days often result in entries having remarkably low risk and a remarkably high probability of a significant continuation. An entry on the close of March 31 led to a drawdown the next day of 77 points, worth $962, before the market continued its upward surge.

There was a further entry signal on the basis of the close on April 11. Given that there were only five net confirming indicators and the previous day had experienced a huge downside reversal, it would have required some courage to enter a new trade here. Although the signal was profitable, there were signs that the market might be approaching the end of its run. The exit checklist for the close of April 10 had a net score of four points in favor of liquidation, which suggested a deteriorating bull market (see completed Form 3).

All contracts were liquidated on the close of April 20, when the signals to liquidate were overwhelming (see completed Form 3). You might have been tempted to re-enter a long position after the upside key reversal and double reversal on April 25. But by that time, sufficient deterioration of the market had occurred that the entry checklist failed to indicate a new buy signal. The checklist was correct: a downside key reversal occurred the next day that would have taken out a stop. In fact, on the basis of the weekly chart, the Japanese Yen had almost lost its qualification as a market to trade on the long side by the close of April 25. %K on the weekly chart topped at 94 on April 7. The only weekly confirming indicator, an old price rule signal, was soon reversed by a price rule sell signal.

The Record

The Japanese Yen's bull move demonstrates how a rapidly moving market is likely to deliver bigger profits faster and with lower risk than most other kinds of market action. You have to find only one or two opportunities like this each year, and trade them conservatively, in order to justify handsomely having a futures account. One key, however, is to have the psychological readiness to enter trades when a market has shown that it can move. You can't have it both ways: a good entry in a market going nowhere is worthless, while a market that has started to move fast is likely to continue, even though it has left its starting point some way behind. Another key, therefore, is to find the few Japanese Yen trades and try to avoid as many small trades as possible in markets having limited potential.

With such a high probability of making profits in a rapidly moving market, this kind of action generally provides the best opportunities for adding contracts on the way. The one prime place to add to the Japanese Yen was on the close of March 31, at 1.1657. However, every Five Star entry signal during the move was profitable.

The summary below shows the results from trading the Japanese Yen, starting with one contract and adding one contract at each new signal. The drawdown column shows the maximum drawdown per trade from entry. The cumulative drawdown column shows the total drawdown as more contracts were added.

Entry Date	Entry Price	Drawdown	Cumulative Drawdown	Exit Date	Exit Price	Profit
March 2	1.0623	$ 537	$ 537	April 20	1.2104	$18,512
March 9	1.1168	2,100	4,200	April 20	1.2104	11,700
March 17	1.1331	1,525	4,575	April 20	1.2104	9,662
March 31	1.1657	962	3,848	April 20	1.2104	5,587
April 11	1.2070	1,500	7,500	April 20	1.2104	425
						$45,886

   In practice, this kind of trading is far too aggressive. The rule for adding is that you should add fewer contracts at each addition to the pyramid. If you started with three contracts for the first entry, you might add one contract with each new entry. Alternatively, if you started with one contract, you might add a half contract on the MidAmerica exchange with each new entry.

Form 2 Five Star ENTRY Checklist

Contract: __JYM '95__ Buy: __✓__ Sell: _____ Date Started: __2/17/95__

	Weekly Chart					Daily Chart						
Confirming Indicators												
Date	2/24	3/17	3/31	4/11	4/25	3/2	3/9	3/17	3/31	4/11		
1. Four-Price Line	✓	✓	✓	✓	✓	✓	✓	✓	✓	✓		
2. Single-Price Line	✓	✓	✓	✓	X	✓	✓	✓	✓	✓		
3. MACD	✓	✓	✓	✓	✓	✓	✓	✓	✓	✓		
4. % K Turn	✓	✓	✓	X	X	✓	X	✓	✓	X		
5. 25- Bar MA Direction	✓	✓	✓	✓	✓	✓	✓	✓	✓	✓		
6. 40-Bar MA Direction	✓	✓	✓	✓	✓	✓	✓	✓	✓	✓		
7. Price Rule Signal	✓	✓	✓	✓		✓	✓	✓	✓	✓		
8. Reversal at MA/Trendline	✓											
9. Key Reversal			✓			✓						
10. Double Reversal							✓					
11. Gap	✓	✓	✓					✓				
12. Island [1]												
Total	9	8	9	6	4	8	7	8	7	6		
Negating Indicators												
1. Adverse %K Level [2]		✓	✓	✓		✓	✓	✓	✓	✓		
2. Adverse Gap(s) [3]												
3. Adverse Breakpoint	✓											
4. Adverse Channel Line												
5. Double Top/Bottom	✓											
6. Adverse Trendline												
Total	2	1	1	1		1	1	1	1	1		
NET CONFIRMING INDICATORS (Confirming – Negating: 5 needed on both weekly & daily for entry)[4]	7	7	8	5		7	6	7	6	5		
Other Indicators												
1. 60-Minute Chart						✓	✓	✓	✓	✓		
2. Commitments of Traders						✓	✓	✓	✓	✓		
3. On Balance Volume	✓	✓	✓	✓		✓	✓	✓	✓	✓		
4. Accumulation/Distribution	✓	✓	✓	✓		✓	✓	✓	✓	✓		
5. Backwardation												
6. Stop/Capital Management						✓	✓	✓	✓	✓		

[1] If an island occurs only on the *daily* chart, also count it on the *weekly* chart.

[2] If %K is >80 or <20 on the weekly chart and/or >70 or <30 on the daily chart, count as a negating indicator.

[3] Enter one check for each adverse gap that remains unfilled on a closing basis during the most recent consolidation.

[4] For a potential *major trend change*, confirming indicators 1, 2, 3, 4 and 7 on the weekly and daily charts should confirm.

Form 3   Five Star EXIT Checklist

Contract: __*JYM '95*__ Long: __✔__ Short: _____ Date Started: __*3/27/95*__

	Weekly Chart					Daily Chart								
Confirming Indicators: Exit														
Date	3/27	4/10	4/20			3/27	4/10	4/20						
1. Four-Price Line	X	X	X			✔	X	✔						
2. Single-Price Line	X	X	X			✔	✔	✔						
3. MACD	X	X	X			✔	X	✔						
4. % K Turn	X	✔	✔			✔	✔	✔						
5. Adverse Price Rule Signal	X	X	X			✔	X	✔						
6. 25-Bar MA Direction	X	X	X			X	X	X						
7. 40-Bar MA Direction	X	X	X			X	X	X						
8. Adverse Trendline Close							✔							
9. Adverse Double Reversal														
10. Adverse Key Reversal														
11. Adverse Gaps: Recent Total						✔①		✔①						
12. Islands (Include. 60-Min. Chart)														
13. %K Level [1]			✔				✔	✔						
14. Adverse Weekly Reversal [2]		✔					✔							
15. At Support or Resistance [3]														
Total	0	2	2			6	4	8						
Negating Indicators: Stay														
1. Favorable Gap(s)								✔						
2. Favorable Breakpoint Holding						✔		✔						
3. Favorable %K Level [1]														
4. Favorable Trendline Holding														
Total						1		2						
NET CONFIRMING INDICATORS (Confirming – Negating: 5 Needed) [4]						5		6						
Other Indicators														
1. 60-Minute Chart	░	░	░	░	░	✔	X	✔						
2. Commitments of Traders	░	░	░	░	░	X	X	✔						
3. On Balance Volume						X	X	X						
4. Accumulation/Distribution						X	X	X						
5. Backwardation	░	░	░	░	░									
6. Stop/Capital Management	░	░	░	░	░	✔	✔	✔						

[1] %K is overbought on the weekly chart at >80 and on the daily chart at >70. It is oversold on the weekly chart at <20 and on the daily chart at <30.

[2] Count on both the weekly and daily charts.

[3] Check the weekly and daily charts for double (or more) adverse tops or bottoms, adverse gaps or breakpoints, channel lines and long-term adverse trendlines, and the daily chart for contract high or low.

[4] When there is a net total of 4 confirming exit indicators on the daily chart, place a tight stop and exit quickly if adverse price action continues, particularly if there is an adverse gap on the next open.

Chapter 22

Case Study: Major Trend Change

It is always worth keeping an eye on markets that have a record of frequent and substantial moves, even when little or nothing appears to be happening. You don't want to miss the next time they spring to life. Cotton is one of those markets that often makes big moves up and down. The first alert to start watching Cotton in 1994 for a potential new bull market occurred as its decline seemed to be rounding out above the support level represented by the high in 1992. This is how the watch unfolded, based on monitoring the prime entry indicators for a potentially emerging bull market (Chapter 16) on the weekly chart from July to October.

Prime Entry Indicators

1. The four-price line on the weekly continuation chart for Cotton (not shown) was in a steady downward zigzag, until it bottomed on October 14. On the weekly chart for the December contract, the low on October 14 held marginally above the low on September 2 (Chart 22.1b). Once the four-price line turned up at a higher level than the previous low on the weekly December chart, and with price at an important support level on the weekly continuation chart, there was a high probability that a new bull market could be starting.

   When there are differences between contracts such as can occur between new and old crop contracts in the grains, we look at both the weekly continuation chart and the weekly chart for the contract month being considered for a trade. Greater weight is given to the latter when there is a conflict.

2. MACD was rounding on both weekly charts and turned up on October 14.

3. %K reached 17 on July 15 on the weekly continuation chart. It made a second low at 18 on August 19 when price was slightly lower and a third low at 23 on October 7 when price was insignificantly lower on the weekly continuation chart, and higher on the December and March daily charts.

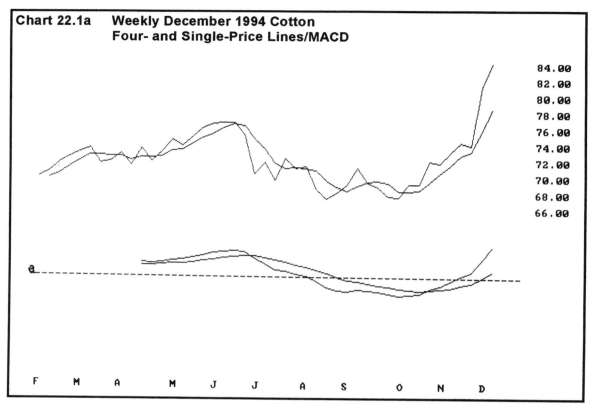

Chart 22.1a   **Weekly December 1994 Cotton**
Four- and Single-Price Lines/MACD

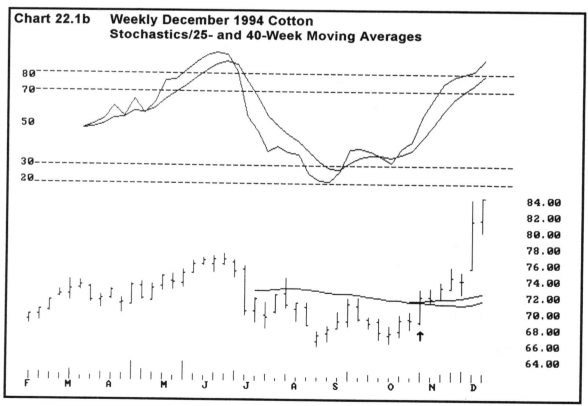

Chart 22.1b   **Weekly December 1994 Cotton**
Stochastics/25- and 40-Week Moving Averages

The significantly higher third low in %K suggested bullish divergence.   %K turned up on October 14 (Chart 22.1b).

4.   The 25-week moving average turned down on July 15 in response to the price decline from the spring high (Chart 22.1b).   The 40-week moving average had been moving higher from early 1994 but by October had turned flat.

5.   Neither a price rule 5 Lindahl nor a rule 8 double reversal buy signal formed on the weekly chart.   But there was a price rule 3, gap buy signal as a result of the gap up on the open and high close for the second bar, for the week ending October 14.

The prime entry indicators suggested that the Cotton market had been experiencing basing action since mid-July.   By the week ending October 14, the four- and single-price lines, MACD and %K had all turned up and a valid price rule signal was completed.   The first five confirming indicators on Form 2, entry checklist therefore gave a buy signal.

Form 2, Entry Checklist

On the December Cotton chart, price started to make a series of small upward gaps and upside reversals on October 6 (Chart 22.2b).   Consequently, Cotton started to be tracked on Form 1, the daily market checklist.   The intraday action on October 24, coupled with a strong upside reversal two days earlier, led to an immediate analysis using Form 2, entry checklist.

The checklist for the December 1994 weekly chart on October 24 showed six net confirming indicators (see completed Form 2, page 158).   The daily checklist had ten strong confirming indicators and three negating ones (see Charts 22.2a and b, and Form 2).   Of the three negating indicators, one was an overbought %K reading of 75, which can be ignored for a market starting to move fast out of a consolidation.   Although there was a gap down from September 16, the power of the confirming indicators suggested that its resistance was likely to be overcome.

On balance volume and accumulation/distribution were particularly interesting and supportive (Chart 22.3).   On October 24 OBV looked ready to break out to a new high.   A/D had made its low in July and had been trending upward since then, despite the bearish price action.

Given the bullish assessment, long positions in Cotton were entered on the close of October 24.   There were several potential entry points after this close (and/or the next day's open).   But none was so prime as the entry the day the market started to move and closed above an important downtrend line.   This demonstrates again that when a strong signal occurs, you must seize the moment.

The Cotton example shows how relatively quickly a market can change from being in the process of making a major trend change to becoming a full-fledged bull market.   It also demonstrates how important it is to monitor a market regularly when the indicators on the weekly chart suggest that a major trend change is under way.

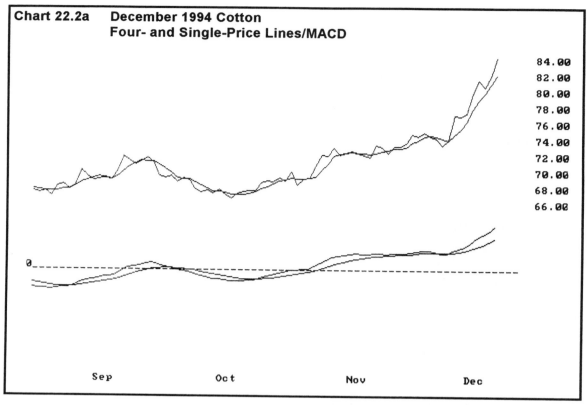

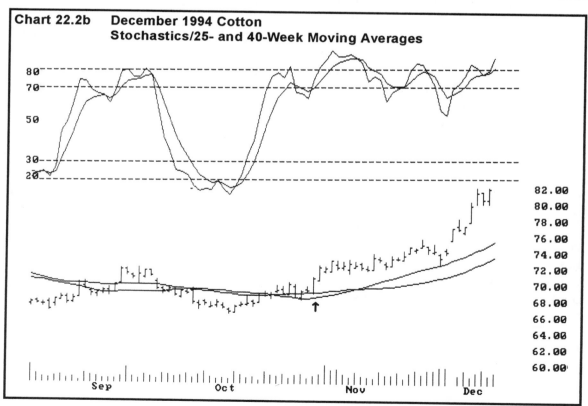

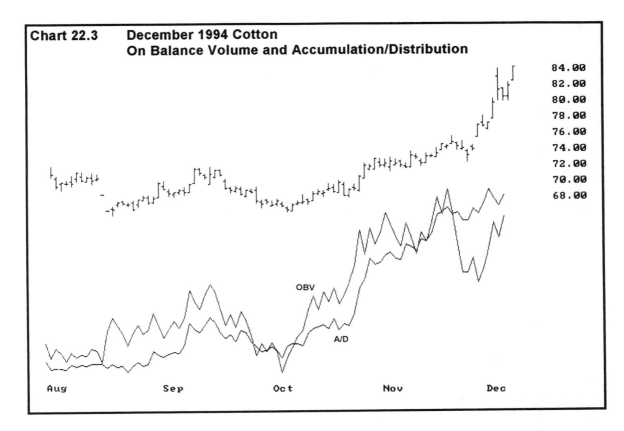

**Chart 22.3 December 1994 Cotton
On Balance Volume and Accumulation/Distribution**

On November 28, about a month after our initial entry, Cotton became a rapidly moving market by gapping up powerfully near the level of the contract high and closing up 300 points, ten points off its high for the day. (December was then trading without limits.) Despite the proximity of the contract high, this move signaled another entry point because of its power and the confirmation of the entry indicators.

Form 2   Five Star ENTRY Checklist

Contract: __CTZ '94__ Buy: __✔__ Sell: _____ Date Started: __10/24/94__

	Weekly Chart (CTZ)				Daily Chart				
Confirming Indicators									
Date	10/24				10/24				
1. Four-Price Line	✔				✔				
2. Single-Price Line	✔				✔				
3. MACD	✔				✔				
4. % K Turn	✔				✔				
5. 25- Bar MA Direction	✗				✔				
6. 40-Bar MA Direction	✔				✔				
7. Price Rule Signal	✔				✔				
8. Reversal at MA/Trendline					✔				
9. Key Reversal					✔				
10. Double Reversal					✔				
11. Gap									
12. Island [1]									
Total	6				10				
Negating Indicators									
1. Adverse %K Level [2]					✔				
2. Adverse Gap(s) [3]					✔ ①				
3. Adverse Breakpoint	✔				✔				
4. Adverse Channel Line									
5. Double Top/Bottom									
6. Adverse Trendline									
Total	1				3				
NET CONFIRMING INDICATORS (Confirming – Negating: 5 needed on both weekly & daily for entry)[4]	5				7				
Other Indicators									
1. 60-Minute Chart					✔				
2. Commitments of Traders					✔				
3. On Balance Volume	✔				✔				
4. Accumulation/Distribution	✔				✔				
5. Backwardation									
6. Stop/Capital Management					✔				

[1] If an island occurs only on the *daily* chart, also count it on the *weekly* chart.

[2] If %K is >80 or <20 on the weekly chart and/or >70 or <30 on the daily chart, count as a negating indicator.

[3] Enter one check for each adverse gap that remains unfilled on a closing basis during the most recent consolidation.

[4] For a potential *major trend change,* confirming indicators 1, 2, 3, 4 and 7 on the weekly and daily charts should confirm.

Chapter 23

The Vacuum Crash

The largest and fastest profits can be made when a bubble bursts at tops. The result of a bubble bursting is what we call a vacuum crash. Some spectacular crashes like the stock market in 1987 or the British Pound in 1992 gain widespread attention. But there are generally a few market collapses each year that are less publicized, although still significant.

When a market crashes from a very high price to a much lower one, it is as if the proverbial rug is pulled out from under that market. A crash occurs either when fundamental reasons for a market being very high, or perceptions of reality, change radically, suddenly and unexpectedly (except for some insiders and some sophisticated speculators).

For example, the British Pound crashed when Britain was forced to withdraw suddenly from the European exchange rate mechanism because the level of interest rates required to keep its currency within the allowable bands surged suddenly to an unsustainable level. Knowledgeable fundamentalists knew that this outcome could occur at some point. Technicians knew from their monthly charts that the Pound had not been able to move above two dollars (the level from which it crashed) since November 1981. Neither group knew when the probable reversal would occur but some positioned themselves early for the expected crash.

In any event, once the fundamentals, or the perceptions that put a market extremely high, suddenly change, there can be a vacuum below the market, with a complete absence of buyers willing to absorb massive selling, which feeds on itself. Hence our term for this kind of trade: vacuum crash.

Prime Vacuum Crash Indicators

The greater the number of prime vacuum crash indicators present, the more likely there is to be a substantial crash.

1. Price is high by historical standards (best checked on monthly charts or in the *CRB Commodity Yearbook*).

2. General euphoria exists, with analysts and news media forecasting further price increases. Comments are often made that the price level is justified

because "things are different this time" and "we've entered a new era". This euphoria is manifested by:

a) a pronounced weighting in the Commitments of Traders data of speculators on the long side and of the commercials on the short side;

b) Bullish Consensus readings currently, or recently, in the range of 80 percent or more; and

c) very high readings on oscillators like stochastics and RSI.

Many traders observe these conditions and attempt to pick a top prematurely. It is worth repeating the adage that bull markets die hard: the mere existence of the above conditions does not necessarily mean that a vacuum crash is imminent. On the contrary, runaway markets often go much farther than you expect and they seldom fall apart without first setting up to do so.

3. There is currently developing, or there has recently been, at least one weekly downside reversal and preferably more, ideally including a weekly price rule 5, Lindahl sell signal.

4. a) An island top occurs on the daily chart (sometimes better seen on the 60-minute chart). The longer it takes to form, the more reliable it is. A clean break between the island top and price action below it is preferable; *or*

b) An extended topping process occurs, ideally with rounding so that the overall appearance of the chart is like a river preparing to go over a waterfall.

5. A strong price rule sell signal is given on the daily chart, ideally with gapping and a very powerful thrust downward. A limit move, where applicable, is the best evidence of the momentum required to break the market.

6. Price breaks down through an uptrend line, where applicable, on a closing basis on the daily chart.

7. Confirmation that the back of the bull market is broken occurs when the market closes decisively below all previous lows made during the past seven weeks.

Vacuum Crash Indicators and Soybeans

It is almost an annual tradition that a weather scare occurs in the grain markets some time during the spring or summer. Most of these scares do not turn into genuine weather markets. But they frequently run prices much higher than is justified by the evolving situation. Thus, overblown expectations of "Beans in the teens" can quickly turn into Soybeans at 5.50. November 1994 Soybeans show a typical bust (Chart 23.2b). At the start of the usual spring rally period in Soybeans, they were at a fairly high level around 6.50. Flooding in the Midwest in 1993 had resulted in a very small crop and a high price of 7.54 (Chart 23.1b). The 1994 spring rally took Soybeans to 7.32 by the week ending May 27. The market then started to fluctuate quite violently. By the week ending June 17 it had rallied back up to 7.15.

Mid-June to early July is frequently a make-or-break period for Soybeans (and Corn) as weather patterns for the summer evolve. It was therefore logical to consider at this point whether price could go higher or whether it had reached a level from which it could only go down. Consequently, for the week ending June 17 we analysed Soybeans in terms of our prime vacuum crash indicators and found the following results.

1. July Soybeans closed the week ending June 17 at 7.11 (Chart 23.2b). The monthly chart in Soybeans (not shown) indicates that a major drought or other unusual circumstances have normally been required to drive price beyond the 7.30 to 7.54 level.

2. Soybeans are one market which seems to generate at least short-lived euphoria almost every year, possibly because it appears to be the favorite market of many of the funds.

    a) Commitments of Traders numbers for June 7 showed non-commercials net long 23 percent, commercials net short 33 percent and small traders net long 10 percent.

    b) Bullish Consensus had been around 70 percent bullish, high but not extremely high.

    c) %K on the weekly chart was only moderately high, at 53, but showed pronounced bearish divergence from its December 31, 1993 high reading of 94. Daily %K was at 78.

3. a) A huge weekly downside reversal occurred the week ending May 27. Price then rebounded powerfully the weeks ending June 10 and 17, and closed near the top of the week's range on June 17 and at major resistance on the weekly chart.

    b) Neither a weekly price rule 5 nor 8 sell signal occurred. But remember that a price rule 5, Lindahl sell signal first requires a decline in price and then a rebound, which can sometimes be so powerful that it is easy to believe that price will continue higher.

4. Neither an island nor an extended topping process occurred on the daily chart. In fact, price gapped up powerfully during the week, tested into the gap and closed near the high of the week. The gap up therefore did not look like an exhaustion gap but only future market action could confirm or deny that possibility.

    The double top on the weekly chart suggested the need to keep in mind the hypothesis that a year-long topping process could be unfolding.

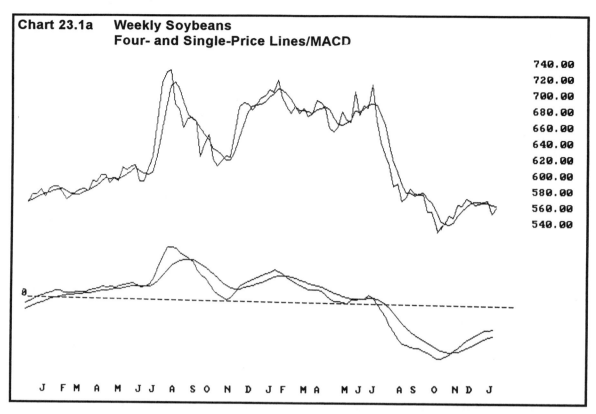

Chart 23.1a   Weekly Soybeans
Four- and Single-Price Lines/MACD

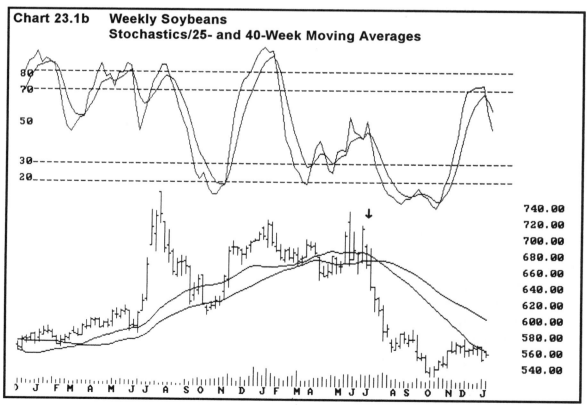

Chart 23.1b   Weekly Soybeans
Stochastics/25- and 40-Week Moving Averages

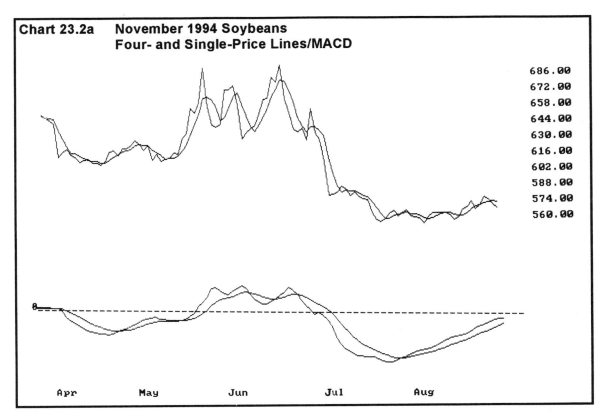

Chart 23.2a   November 1994 Soybeans
Four- and Single-Price Lines/MACD

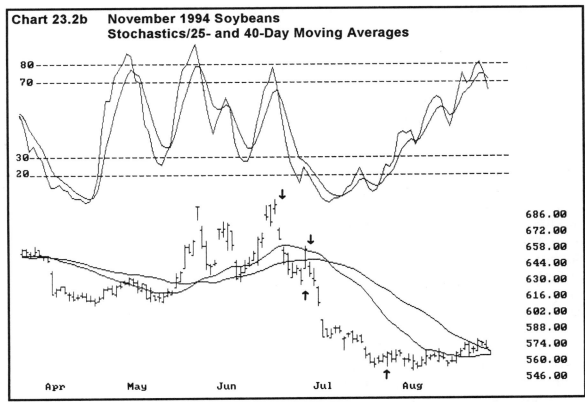

Chart 23.2b   November 1994 Soybeans
Stochastics/25- and 40-Day Moving Averages

5.   On June 17 price went to a new contract high and closed 1.75 points higher than the previous high close. Therefore, the only possibility of a near-term sell signal would be if an island formed with a powerful downside thrust (a price rule 4, island sell signal). That action could also result in a weekly Lindahl sell signal.

6.   To make a new seven-week low in order to confirm that the back of the bull was broken, the market would need to close below the low of the week of May 13 at 6.10.

We drew three conclusions from our review of the prime vacuum crash indicators:

1.   On the face of it, recent daily price action looked extremely bullish. But price was in the range where it had historically turned back, barring a major disaster. Therefore, price could be forming a top.

2.   Price action had been violent for a month and would probably continue to be. This meant that an entry into the market, particularly a short sale, would probably have to be done very quickly, almost as an automatic response to certain conditions.

3.   Price action—the market itself—would show us what to do, if anything. For a short sale, including a potential vacuum crash, we had to see the possibility of a sell signal on the weekly chart (probably a Lindahl sell signal) and a gap open—the bigger, the better, and preferably one creating an island.

Trading a Vacuum Crash

On the next trading day, Monday, June 20, pre-opening calls were for a substantially lower open in Soybeans. This meant that there would be a stochastic/gap sell signal that required the liquidation on the open of any long positions we might have held. It also meant that the signals we were looking for to trigger a short sale—a gap opening, an island and a potential weekly Lindahl sell signals—were all real possibilities. In fact, Soybeans opened at 6.73, 22 points under the previous close, leaving an island on the daily chart and potentially producing a price rule 5, Lindahl sell signal on the weekly chart.

The preferred approach for handling entries in markets like November Soybeans is to put on a short position in two steps. The first step is to enter an order before the market opens, or immediately after the open if there is doubt about the pre-opening call. Then you will be filled on all except the rare occasions when a market goes immediately to limit down and jams there. That seldom happens on the first day of a market break.

The second order should go in as the market heads toward limit down, by stop if you like. If trading only a single contract, a sale into limit down generally runs a lower risk of a rebound than a sale made at a higher price. Limit moves scare holders of long positions, thereby setting the stage for panic liquidation. If the market locks at limit down, the follow-through the next day should be almost automatic.

In a situation such as November Soybeans, it not possible to wait until late in the day to complete the entry checklist because the market may lock at limit down well before the close. Instead, you must be sure that the conditions for a vacuum crash exist and that the entry signals you identified as necessary to sell short are unfolding. If this is the case, you can assume that the indicators on the entry checklist will also confirm the trade. A Form 2 for November Soybeans completed on the close of June 20 (page 167), and Charts 23.2a and (b), demonstrate this contention.

The persistent non-confirmation by accumulation/distribution of the bull market in Soybeans is worth noting, particularly since on balance volume remained strong throughout May and June (Chart 23.3). The big surge in OBV at the top, when not confirmed by A/D, suggested that Soybeans were subject to a buying frenzy that was unlikely to last.

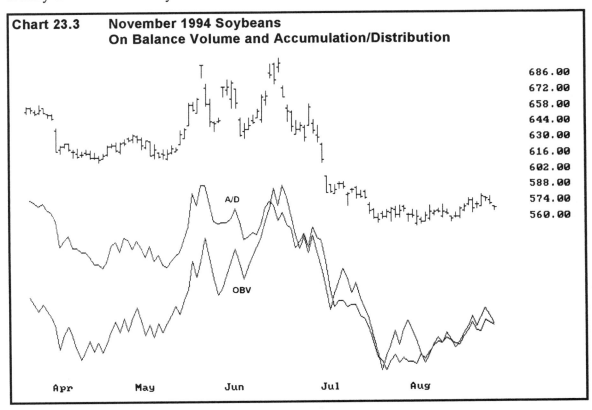

**Chart 23.3   November 1994 Soybeans
On Balance Volume and Accumulation/Distribution**

Just as you have to be ready to enter a trade when there is a prime opportunity, you must be equally alert to the possibility of a rebound against an existing trade. On the second day of the Soybean trade, price went down 22 points and then rebounded to close in the upper half of the day's range. Stops were therefore based on a stop rule 4, inside limit move, resulting in a new stop each day 15 points above the previous day's low. The stop for June 28 was placed at 6.41 and the trade was stopped out just after the open.

A failed limit move rally occurred on June 28, which signaled the possibility of the downtrend resuming as early as the next day. We therefore placed a sell stop at 6.39, just below the low of June 28 and were filled. It would also have been possible to sell short into the close on June 29 at 6.35. After this entry, price plunged down to a new seven-week low and then moved steadily lower over the next few weeks.

Market action suggested the need to run through the exit checklist on July 13 and July 26. As the completed Form 3 indicates (page 168), only the last of these checks resulted in a net total of five indicators to confirm liquidation.

The results of the vacuum crash trades are shown below.

Entry Date	Long/Short	Entry Price	Exit Date	Exit Price	Profit/Loss
June 20	Short	665.00	June 28	641.00	$1,200
June 29	Short	639.00	July 26	566.50	3,625
					$4,825

The total profit before commissions and slippage of $4,825 was booked over a period of just six weeks with only one contract for each of the two entries.

Form 2   Five Star ENTRY Checklist

Contract: __SX '94__   Buy: _____   Sell: __✔__   Date Started: __6/20/94__

	Weekly Chart					Daily Chart						
Confirming Indicators												
Date	6/20					6/20	6/29					
1. Four-Price Line	✔					✔	✔					
2. Single-Price Line	✔					✔	✔					
3. MACD	✔					✔	✔					
4. % K Turn	✔					✔	✔					
5. 25- Bar MA Direction	✔					X	✔					
6. 40-Bar MA Direction	X					X	X					
7. Price Rule Signal	✔					✔	✔					
8. Reversal at MA/Trendline												
9. Key Reversal												
10. Double Reversal												
11. Gap	✔					✔	✔					
12. Island [1]						✔	✔					
Total	7					7	8					
Negating Indicators												
1. Adverse %K Level [2]							✔					
2. Adverse Gap(s) [3]												
3. Adverse Breakpoint												
4. Adverse Channel Line												
5. Double Top/Bottom												
6. Adverse Trendline												
Total	0					0	1					
NET CONFIRMING INDICATORS (Confirming – Negating: 5 needed on both weekly & daily for entry)[4]	7					7	7					
Other Indicators												
1. 60-Minute Chart						✔	✔					
2. Commitments of Traders						✔	✔					
3. On Balance Volume	X					✔	X					
4. Accumulation/Distribution	X						X					
5. Backwardation												
6. Stop/Capital Management						✔	✔					

[1]   If an island occurs only on the *daily* chart, also count it on the *weekly* chart.

[2]   If %K is >80 or <20 on the weekly chart and/or >70 or <30 on the daily chart, count as a negating indicator.

[3]   Enter one check for each adverse gap that remains unfilled on a closing basis during the most recent consolidation.

[4]   For a potential *major trend change*, confirming indicators 1, 2, 3, 4 and 7 on the weekly and daily charts should confirm.

Form 3   Five Star EXIT Checklist

Contract: __SX '94__   Long:_____   Short: _✓_   Date Started: __7/26__

Confirming Indicators: Exit	Weekly Chart					Daily Chart					
Date	7/13	7/26				7/13	7/26				
1. Four-Price Line	X	X				✓	✓				
2. Single-Price Line	X	X				✓	✓				
3. MACD	X	X				X	✓				
4. % K Turn	X	X				✓	✓				
5. Adverse Price Rule Signal	X	X				✓	✓				
6. 25-Bar MA Direction	X	X				X	X				
7. 40-Bar MA Direction	X	X				X	X				
8. Adverse Trendline Close							✓				
9. Adverse Double Reversal											
10. Adverse Key Reversal							✓				
11. Adverse Gaps: Recent Total						✓①	✓⓪				
12. Islands (Include. 60-Min. Chart)											
13. %K Level [1]		✓				✓					
14. Adverse Weekly Reversal [2]											
15. At Support or Resistance [3]		✓									
Total	0	2				6	8				
Negating Indicators: Stay											
1. Favorable Gap(s)						✓					
2. Favorable Breakpoint Holding						✓					
3. Favorable %K Level [1]											
4. Favorable Trendline Holding											
Total						2	0				
NET CONFIRMING INDICATORS (Confirming – Negating: 5 Needed) [4]						4	8				
Other Indicators											
1. 60-Minute Chart	▓	▓	▓	▓	▓	✓	✓				
2. Commitments of Traders	▓	▓	▓	▓	▓	X	X				
3. On Balance Volume						X	✓				
4. Accumulation/Distribution						X	✓				
5. Backwardation	▓	▓	▓	▓	▓						
6. Stop/Capital Management	▓	▓	▓	▓	▓	✓	✓				

[1]   %K is overbought on the weekly chart at >80 and on the daily chart at >70. It is oversold on the weekly chart at <20 and on the daily chart at <30.

[2]   Count on both the weekly and daily charts.

[3]   Check the weekly and daily charts for double (or more) adverse tops or bottoms, adverse gaps or breakpoints, channel lines and long-term adverse trendlines, and the daily chart for contract high or low.

[4]   When there is a net total of 4 confirming exit indicators on the daily chart, place a tight stop and exit quickly if adverse price action continues, particularly if there is an adverse gap on the next open.

Chapter 24

The End of the Beginning

We have led you step-by-step through the Five Star system. Now it is your turn: to learn it and to apply it. To help you, this chapter discusses some non-technical points relevant to learning and using the system.

Learning to trade a futures trading system is no different from learning any other fairly complex skill, whether it is a new job or playing golf well. They all require hard work, continued practice, the ability to recover from inevitable set-backs....You, in fact, know what it takes to master a new job or to play golf or another sport at a competent level. Trading futures is no different.

After the first reading of the book, you may find it useful to review the ideas in each chapter by analysing old and current charts. Check to see how the signals we look for do occur and do signal good trades. Chapter 16, with its summaries of the prime entry indicators for established trends, rapidly moving markets and major trend changes, might help you to ease into the full use of all the components of the system.

Before you can successfully trade a system, you must not only know it but feel intellectually and psychologically comfortable with it. Therefore, before proceeding to real trades, you should make real-time trading decisions on paper. Real-time paper trading will sharpen your ability to recognize and act on trading signals as they occur. It should also help you learn to trust the signals the system gives—and to trust yourself using it. This aspect is critical if you are to have the courage to act on your convictions. Without this ability, you are unlikely to be able to trade successfully over the long-term.

You may have to work at and practice some or all of the following important aspects of trading. This list is not inclusive but it will give you lots to think about!

1. *Looking for good Five Star signals:* These are the trades that "add up" on Form 2, entry checklist (and the higher the score the better).

2. *Avoiding overtrading,* which is related to the first point: Some people feel that they must be trading at all times and/or in many markets at the same time. This approach will inevitably result in taking some inferior trades and, as a

result, being diverted from some good trades because your money and attention are tied up nursing poor performers.

3.   *Taking signals when they are given*:   The best trades will often not give a second opportunity to enter at as good a price.   Also, if you wait and then enter a trade after the market has moved considerably, the risk inevitably increases.

The corollary of this point is: don't trade at all when there are no valid signals to take!

4.   *Using stops*:   It is important to place stops in accordance with what the system specifies rather than with what your entry price suggests.   The market neither knows nor cares where you traded in.   It is sometimes right to place stops to protect commissions.   But a trade should normally be allowed to fluctuate within the tolerances allowed by the system, even if this means letting a trade go back and forth between a profit and a loss.

Virtually everyone finds that the time of greatest stress in a trade is the period before a cushion of profit is established.   It is extremely easy to liquidate good trades prematurely because of concerns about whether they are making money or not, rather than to consider whether the signal to trade remains valid.

5.   *Managing your capital*:   The foremost objective is keeping your account in business.   That means not overtrading or exceeding the amount of equity allowable for any trade, however strong its signals or however good its apparent merits.

The possibilities in favor of making profits over time deteriorate dramatically when more equity is used on a single trade than allows for a ten percent loss of equity if the stop is hit.   Sometimes the merits of a trade are so overwhelming that everyone can see them and there is no one left to push the market further.   That is when the biggest market accidents generally occur.

6.   *Re-entering a previously traded market*:   The biggest market moves usually generate many trades, although not all of them will necessarily be profitable. Sometimes the requirements of capital management dictate the liquidation of a trade at a loss, whether by stop or by exit signal, rather than tolerating a retracement that could get out of hand.   In this case, guard against psychologically throwing up your hands and assuming that you cannot or should not re-enter. The best part may remain to come.

Even the best bull or bear markets may have major washouts because price has gone too far too quickly or the trade has become too popular. (Remember the relevance of Commitments of Traders in this connection.)

7.   *Coping with losses*:   Losses are an inherent part of futures trading, as they are of almost every business.   By extension, account drawdowns are normal, up to a point, and therefore must not be allowed to affect your ability to make good decisions.

Losses can be destabilising and can unconsciously lead to making bad trading decisions. After losses, people often decide to trade conservatively. But this strategy can be counter-productive if it takes any form other than scaling back on commitments to the market. Attempting to trade conservatively can be disastrous if it leads you to take weak signals in listless markets, resulting in a succession of whipsaws.

8. *Having the courage of your convictions*: Many factors can shake your confidence in a trade, whether you are already in it or only thinking of taking it. For example, if you receive any news services, you will be exposed to the views of a wide range of "experts", "analysts" and "traders". These views may be the opposite of your own and may be endlessly repeated as received wisdom. In such circumstances, remember that the people quoted may well have analytical tools inferior to your own. Or they may not be sincere in their stated views but merely trying to set up a market to enter at a better price themselves.

The best antidote to any factor that shakes your confidence in a trade is to review its merits by carefully and objectively working through the entry checklist and/or the exit checklist again. As well, go through this book from time-to-time to refresh your memory; it is very easy to forget important concepts.

And now, it's over to you. You are at the end of your new beginning in trading futures. Good luck comes to those who make it happen!

See the Five Star system in action!

If you would like to see how someone else uses the Five Star system, or if you prefer to have someone else do the day-to-day homework, you are invited to contact the author's advisory service:

The Wellspring Futures Newsletter
P.O. Box 7243
Ottawa, Ontario   K1L 8E3
Canada

Telephone: (613) 745-5593
Fax: (613) 745-1156